Science Education Through Multiple Literacies

Science Education Through Multiple Literacies

Project-Based Learning in Elementary School

Edited by
JOSEPH KRAJCIK
BARBARA SCHNEIDER

HARVARD EDUCATION PRESS
CAMBRIDGE, MA

Paperback ISBN 978-1-68253-662-9

Library of Congress Cataloging-in-Publication Data is on file.

Published by Harvard Education Press,
an imprint of the Harvard Education Publishing Group
Harvard Education Press
8 Story Street
Cambridge, MA 02138

Cover Design: Wilcox Design
Cover Image: SDI Productions/E+ via Getty Images

The typefaces in this book are Adobe Garamond Pro and Myriad Pro.

Contents

Foreword

Young children are great scientists. They love to understand nature, to compare and contrast, to try things out and test new ideas, to figure out cause and effect. They take nothing for granted, are always ready not just to learn but also to unlearn and relearn when new paradigms emerge. And when they have discovered something new, they immediately take ownership of that and are eager to tell the whole world about it.

But as children grow older, many turn away from this early love, considering the natural sciences to be an abstract world of formulas and equations that is unrelated to their lives and dreams.

A lot of that has to do with how we learn and teach science. What students learn in school science is often a mile wide but just an inch deep, quickly memorized and then forgotten, and unrelated to the world around them. Amid all the facts and figures learned in school, it is easy to lose sight of what it means to think like a scientist, to build a hypothesis, to design an experiment, or to distinguish questions that are scientifically investigable from those that are not.

Science Education Through Multiple Literacies seeks to change that, drawing on project-based learning methods that engage elementary students in understanding the nature of science through investigating phenomena, collaborating with their classmates, and building artifacts that demonstrate systems thinking and cause-and-effect reasoning. What this volume adds to the literature is to build scientific foundations around this approach to project-based learning. Many consider education an art, with talented and passionate educators making tremendous efforts each day to teach our children and build our future. But good education requires more than that. It too benefits from scientific exploration, testing novel questions and ideas, and discovering what produces the outcomes we seek. The book uses science to understand how children learn science, and then builds both an evidence base and practical techniques that help educators shift away from teaching the way that they were taught and toward how scientific research teaches us to teach science. This is not presented as gray theory but illustrated by the work of nine innovative teachers whose work focuses on active learning in interactive environments in which students learn through exploration and discovery, build connections between science and the real world, and discover cause-and-effect relationships the way that scientists do.

There is no doubt that traditional science teaching has been successful in attracting and developing an elite who were able to change the world as scientists and engineers. But the challenge is now different. Virtually all of the major challenges facing individuals and nations now require a deep scientific understanding by entire populations. So the future of science teaching is a practice that needs to reach everyone, not just a narrow elite, and this requires a different approach. Appreciating how science has contributed—and can contribute—to the improvement of health, energy and food supply, and adaptability to climate change are all important outcomes for tomorrow's science education. Understanding the different mechanisms that result in particular events and the extent to which these are caused by scientific, social, economic, and political dimensions will empower young people to thrive within complex systems, to identify adequate solutions to problems by evaluating their relative strengths and weaknesses, and to weigh different courses of action on the basis of ethical and economic advantages and disadvantages. Not least, it will enable them to see the physical, ecological, and sociopolitical feedback mechanisms and behaviors that occur because of the connections within a system.

Advancements in technology—in particular, artificial intelligence and biotechnology—add further layers of complexity to decision making. Science education plays a key role in ensuring that young people are equipped to apply ethical reasoning in relation to science, to consider consequences, and evaluate externality in relation to experimental design and problem analysis. It will also help them to accept that science does not give direct answers for decision making or about "what one should do," but requires an ethical and value-driven component. These days, education is no longer just about teaching people something, but about helping them develop a reliable compass and the tools to navigate with confidence through a world that is increasingly complex, increasingly volatile, and increasingly uncertain.

Science education needs not just to equip young people with decision-making competencies to navigate life, but also to empower and support them to take action and "create new value." Schools need to do better in helping students develop a sense of self-efficacy, agency, and responsibility. Only in this way can young people unleash their knowledge and energy to build sustainable cities, start sustainable businesses, push the innovation frontier for green technologies, rethink individual lifestyles, back ecologically responsible policy making, and most importantly, strike the right balance between meeting the needs of the present and safeguarding the ability of future generations to meet their own needs. When young people create new value, they ask questions, collaborate, and try to think outside the box. They approach problems using a range of strategies, reflect on what has and has not worked, and have the resilience and agility to try again in search of a solution. In doing so, they can become more prepared and resilient when confronted with uncertainty and change. The project-based approach to science learning embodied in the case studies presented in this volume reflect this approach to science learning.

The months of the COVID-19 pandemic have brought home the urgency of this approach. During this time, we could all feel the powerful forces of science and Mother Nature. Those who remained ignorant of science or gave precedence to comfortable beliefs, ideology, or politics have paid a steep price for that. We cannot sweet-talk Mother Nature, and we cannot spin her. Mother Nature always follows the principles of science, so we had better help young people thoroughly understand these.

An excellent education in science, building itself on a foundation of the education sciences, will serve the hopes and aspirations of individuals, economies, and nations. It will improve and save many lives and is one of the great investments a society can make in its people and its future. This volume gives us powerful tools for doing that well.

Andreas Schleicher
Director for Education and Skills and Special Advisor
on Education Policy to the Secretary-General
Organisation for Economic Co-operation and Development, Paris

Preface

How can we transform science teaching to support young children to enjoy science, see the wonders of the natural world, and learn challenging ideas that form the foundation for making sense of scientific phenomena? What support can we provide elementary teachers to transform their teaching practice in science? Never before in our society has there been such a great need to shift the teaching and learning of science so that students can use their knowledge to solve community and global problems. Creating a sustainable planet with plentiful healthy food and clean air and fresh water for all individuals throughout the world is imperative. The importance of learning how to solve and respond to new health issues—such as a pandemic—and to understand and trust in science has never been more obvious. Every person needs to recognize the importance of evidence in making scientific claims, while simultaneously realizing that ideas in science can change as new evidence is brought forward.

Science Education Through Project-Based Learning presents case studies of teachers coming to learn how to enact project-based learning (PBL) to engage elementary students. Paralleling what scientists do, PBL represents the essence of doing science as children and their teachers investigate real-world questions, construct models to make sense of phenomena and use evidence to support claims. PBL engages students in understanding the natural world through answering questions related to phenomena, collaborating with their classmates, and building artifacts that demonstrate systems thinking and cause-and-effect reasoning.

Multiple-Literacies in Project Learning (ML-PBL) builds on foundational principles of how students learn. The teaching and student materials are aimed at engaging children in learning goals linked to the Next Generation Science Standards (NGSS) and Common Core State Standards for ELA/Literacy, which are also adopted as the Michigan Standards. Through ML-PBL experiences, students explain phenomena, design solutions to problems, and acquire the intellectual tools to access additional knowledge when needed. Using three-dimensional scientific knowledge (disciplinary core ideas, crosscutting concepts, and science and engineering practices)—as described in the National Research Council's *Framework for K–12 Science Education* and the NGSS performance expectations—requires different instructional practices and ways of thinking about what it means to learn. Through ML-PBL, teachers have students share their artifacts with classmates, family members, and members of their community. By developing a wide supportive community, ML-PBL experiences provide learners with useful feedback and knowledge-building experiences.

ML-PBL is about more than just teaching and student materials. It also consists of long-term professional learning (PL) and assessment tasks that further push student learning. Our PL allows teachers and ML-PBL researchers alike to form a community of learners who benefit from one another's experience and expertise. Our assessment tasks engage them in using the three dimensions of scientific knowledge described in the *Framework*.

The case studies presented here provide vivid portraits of ML-PBL teachers' experiences with their third-grade classes—illustrating the challenges, joys, and reflections on their teaching practices as they come to learn how to enact PBL in their classrooms. The cases present narratives from nearly two hundred classroom observations, video analysis of classroom enactments, student and teacher interviews, social and emotional learning surveys, student artifacts, pre- and post-tests, and summative assessments. The examples and quotations in the book are from the teachers in the study, although at times they were edited for clarity.

Chapter 1 provides an overview of PBL, the development of the ML-PBL materials, and the context in which the case studies took place. Chapters 2 through 10 present the case studies that provide rich images of teachers as they learn and enact ML-PBL practices. The cases show how students, some of whom are struggling learners, come to engage in doing science as a result of experiencing phenomena firsthand. They show the impact PBL has on students' sense-making and on how they collaborate with each other, design and build artifacts, and acquire academic, social, and emotional learning in their science classes. Chapter 11 discusses and demonstrates how the enactment of ML-PBL can fundamentally transform science teaching and learning.

The redesign of teaching practices is not an easy endeavor; however, these cases show how the teachers became more proficient with project-based learning, using new teaching practices to support students in making sense of phenomena or solving meaningful and complex problems. We designed and tested ML-PBL with the hope of transforming the teaching and learning of elementary science instruction so that teachers and children alike would experience and find joy in doing science. The ultimate goal is that teachers and children are empowered to explore their natural world and continue to learn throughout their lives to make informed decisions, supported by evidence so that all people live in a sustainable, free, and peaceful world.

CHAPTER 1

Transforming the Teaching and Learning of Science Through Project-Based Learning

JOSEPH KRAJCIK, EMILY C. ADAH MILLER, AND BARBARA SCHNEIDER

> When I first started teaching project-based learning science, I slowly started incorporating small changes in my teaching. Now it has affected all my teaching, [and] it gave me something to present to the students that was meaningful. I started off with one question; and before long, the class and I were building on another question and then another using the previous knowledge, and soon they were discovering new questions and ideas on their own. At first it was weird, all that questioning, but soon I started to notice that I was doing it in math and reading. Asking different types of questions: "Why do you think this?" "Why do you think things are like this?" "Tell me more; tell me what you mean by this?" Things that I never asked before. This program teaches kids how to think, makes them aware of things around them, questions how they can change things, and what has to happen to make a change. I guess, basically, this experience has opened up the way I teach, and the students feel their ideas are important and valued and are willing to engage in their learning even more.
>
> —MR. STARR

How can we design instructional materials to support teachers in promoting deep academic learning and social and emotional learning? What are critical features that all learning experiences need? How do we engage children in learning about science? This book, based on a systems approach to teaching elementary science, presents the story of Multiple Literacies in Project-Based Learning (ML-PBL) and describes the experiences of third-grade teachers as they learn to support all students in developing science knowledge to make sense of their world.[1] The literature shows that knowing more is not enough for the twenty-first century: students need to know how to use their knowledge. Teachers need to engage learners in experiences that are relevant and meaningful, giving them opportunities to figure out phenomena and work collaboratively to create models and solve problems.

Drawing from a wealth of data gathered over the course of several years—including observations, interviews, surveys, and student artifacts—this book details the successes and challenges teachers encountered as they enacted new teaching practices with ML-PBL. This approach is grounded in usable and adaptable materials for teachers and students, sustained professional learning, and assessments that prepare teachers to support students in developing science understanding and social and emotional learning (SEL). The case studies in this book present the stories of nine teachers as they come to learn how to enact project-based learning to promote academic and social and emotional learning for all students.[2]

AN OVERVIEW OF PROJECT-BASED LEARNING

ML-PBL is based on the principles of project-based learning (PBL). With its focus on students investigating questions that they find meaningful, PBL has the potential to transform classrooms into environments where students work together to generate knowledge and solve worthwhile problems. PBL aligns with recent efforts focusing on reforming K–12 science education that have placed significant attention on what students should know and be able to do with their knowledge.[3] What has received less emphasis is how to accomplish these ambitious reform efforts in classrooms, including the experiences students should have to increase their knowledge, interest, and engagement in science learning.

PBL advances science teaching and learning by immersing students in Driving Questions, investigations, and collaboration to construct knowledge and create artifacts. Stemming from the seminal work of John Dewey, PBL has long been recognized as a viable instructional method that supports student motivation and interest in wondering about their natural world.[4] It engages students in the exploration and explanation of events related to phenomena and developing solutions to real-world problems.

When school science is too much like work, it becomes drudgery, and students are not motivated to do it. We prefer to make school more like playing basketball, volleyball, the guitar, or the piano. It takes considerable effort to become a good volleyball or guitar player, but young children play volleyball or the guitar for hours and often do not need to be told to do so. They choose to do it because they find the activity rewarding. We need to instill that same motivation for learning in all children. One way to make that happen is to make science relevant to students' lives, where they can ask their own questions and engage in finding solutions to those questions they find important. When learners have a personal investment in trying to make sense of phenomena or respond to meaningful questions collaboratively, science in school becomes more like playing a sport or an instrument. Just like children who gradually become proficient in sports and music when practicing at their own level, children in a PBL environment engage in deep knowledge of science ideas and practices tailored to their own developmental level; in turn, they exercise agency to explore relevant questions and problems they experience in their lives.[5]

Projects Start with a Driving Question

PBL starts with the Driving Question that students find meaningful and propels a learning unit forward. It is the initial vehicle for establishing the relevance of science to students' lives and it is this relevance that engages students to sustain their efforts in making sense of the question. An example of a Driving Question is, *Why do I see so many squirrels but can't find any stegosauruses?*.[6] The Driving Question sets the stage for planning, investigating, and artifact development throughout the unit. Because the Driving Question creates a sense of interest, agency, and investment in the explorations that students carry out, the learning environment is markedly transformed. A PBL environment looks and feels different from what typically occurs in an elementary science classroom: it supports learning environments where students become knowledge builders rather than repositories of memorized knowledge. Driving Questions, when designed well, help create a new culture in classrooms where students actively explore, build meaning, and share ideas and questions.[7]

Projects Focus on Performance Learning Goals

A second feature of PBL is performance-based learning goals that guide teaching and learning. The Driving Question serves as an on-ramp to addressing disciplinary *learning goals* that spark how the students build on their understandings and develop creative and collaborative artifacts.[8] As students develop a deeper understanding of the phenomenon under study, their application of the disciplinary ideas and practices becomes more sophisticated. One of the performance learning goals of the Squirrels Unit has the students engage with the question, *How is the squirrel's structure unique and important?* By engaging and answering this question, they meet the performance learning goal, *Students will develop claims with evidence that the squirrel's structures are related to its survival in its environment.*

Scientific Practices to Make Sense of Phenomena

When students engage in PBL, they use scientific practices to investigate phenomena. They ask and seek answers to questions; make predictions; design plans for investigations; measure, collect, and analyze data and/or information; construct models and develop explanations; communicate their ideas and findings to others; and develop and ask new questions. In other words, they continually engage in using science and engineering practices.

In the second unit, the Toys Unit—which focuses on forces and motion—the students engage in artifact development and several different experiments. They are working on answering the Driving Question, *How can we design fun moving toys that any kid can build?* Students begin by exploring a variety of toy air rockets, observing their kinetics, and brainstorming questions about why they move the way they do. The students then take part in a series of investigations to analyze and interpret data, support their claims with evidence and reasoning, and build models that provide causal accounts for phenomena. The unit progresses with students engineering a new toy. PBL, with its emphasis on answering a complex question over time, supports students in connecting scientific practices and ideas, rather than short-term activities that are not relevant to their lives. Engaging in a sustained investigation is a hallmark of doing science, and it supports learners in building knowledge they can use.

Students Engage in Collaborative Activities

PBL parallels the investigative teams of scientists and engineers by giving students opportunities to collaborate on finding solutions to challenging science, medical, and engineering problems facing society. Students collaborate with others and with their teachers to make sense of data and information, build and revise models based on evidence, make claims supported by evidence, and present findings. This is a joint intellectual effort of students, peers, teachers, and community members to figure out a question or problem. When students work with others in this way, they form a community of knowledge builders. PBL is designed to have students work with one another to test their ideas and build meaning. This meaning-making is the underlying characteristic of a community of learners.

For example, in the Squirrels Unit, the students—with support from their teacher—use their observations to build a consensus model that provides an account of how a squirrel uses its unique structures to survive. Collaborating together to build a model, the student and teachers form a knowledge community, which also encourages students to challenge and support their ideas and argue from evidence.

Scaffolds to Support Students Engagement

While making sense of the Driving Question, students are challenged to participate in tasks that might normally be beyond their abilities. The ML-PBL materials therefore offer scaffolds that teachers can use to assist struggling students to engage in the application of science ideas through scientific practices. These scaffolds are critical to PBL because they allow all learners to take part in practices such as constructing models to provide causal explanations of phenomena and making claims supported by evidence and scientific ideas.

Again taking the Squirrels Unit as an example, the students first make observations of squirrels and then create a list of what squirrels need to survive. Because this is the children's first experience building a model, once the list is generated, the teachers task the students to "make a picture" with a partner that shows how the squirrel meets one of those survival needs. The series of learning scaffolds—of creating a list, drawing with a partner, and focusing on one need—supports third-graders in building the model.

Creating a Set of Tangible Artifacts

In PBL, students collaboratively develop artifacts: a series of tangible products that represent their emerging understanding and responses to the Driving Question. The artifacts are ultimately presented to the class or a larger community. Artifact development motivates students to stay sustained in knowledge construction for long periods of time. Because they are tangible objects, they offer students a direct application for their science understanding, providing a bridge between what the student knows and the experience of making the artifact.

Artifacts such as models, reports, and videos are critical to learning for three reasons. First, they act as a mirror to show students their emerging and collective knowledge, are concrete and explicit, and can be shared and critiqued with others in the community. Second, when students build an artifact, the act of creating helps them to see new connections and build deeper knowledge. Third, artifacts can be used for assessment purposes. Models are a representation of what the students know. Often, teachers have students share their artifacts with other classes, parents, and members of the community, who provide feedback to the learners. Such feedback supports learners in reflecting, extending their understanding, and revising their artifacts.

In the Birds Unit, with the overall Driving Question of *How can we help the birds near our school grow up and thrive?* students explore the sub-question: *What kinds of birds live near our playground?* To find an answer, students construct maps of where they have observed different species of birds near the school. They then compare their maps with those of other students in the class (making the investigation authentic and motivating). By comparing and contrasting their maps, students construct new knowledge. They might discover that the area around their school provides several different types of habitats for birds (such as yards, fields, wetlands, and wooded areas) and that specific birds are more frequently seen in particular habitats. The Driving Question in the Birds Unit provides flexibility for students who live in urban, rural, and suburban districts, and is thus responsive and relevant for all students.

FROM PROJECT-BASED LEARNING PRINCIPLES TO MULTIPLE LITERACY IN PROJECT-BASED LEARNING

The transformations in teaching practices that are necessary for enacting PBL do not come easily, and adhering to its principles is challenging. Careful sequencing of tasks across time is needed, as well as scaffolding for students to adopt new ways to learn. Integrated PBL instruction challenges teachers both to enact new instructional practices that support students in developing understanding of rigorous content and to integrate science, literacy, and mathematics into their teaching. To meet these needs, a team with diverse experience and expertise was brought together to design, develop, test, and revise a system for advancing science teaching and learning that builds a vision for enacting PBL that aligns with current reform efforts in the US and internationally.[9]

ML-PBL has developed into a system of: (1) highly developed and specified teacher materials (i.e., how to promote discourse, use of the Driving Questions, a coherent sequence of lessons, scaffolds for developing scientific practices) and highly developed and specified student materials (i.e., hands-on investigations, complex and compiling phenomena, model development, materials for artifact construction, and reading and writing experiences that are integrated with science ideas); (2) professional learning supports (i.e., face-to-face meetings, video conferences, and pedagogical supports related to ongoing learning and specific to each unit); and (3) performance-based informal, formative, and end-of-unit assessments. Additionally, ML-PBL provides mechanisms for ongoing communications with school, district, and intermediate school district leaders.

Promoting Deep Knowledge

Learning and cognitive scientists have made tremendous breakthroughs in understanding how children learn science.[10] Syntheses of publications argue that productive twenty-first-century global citizens need to develop deep knowledge of the big ideas of science by applying and using ideas to explain phenomena and solve problems important to them.[11] Deep knowledge means that ideas are linked to allow learners to access and use them for problem-solving and decision-making and for advancing additional learning.[12] The National Research Council's *A Framework for K–12 Science Education* presents a new vision of science education that moves classroom teaching away from the presentation of disconnected and discrete science facts to learning environments where students use disciplinary core ideas (DCIs), science and engineering practices (SEPs), and crosscutting concepts (CCCs) to make sense of phenomena or design solutions to problems.[13] This integration of the three dimensions is referred to as *three-dimensional learning*.[14]

DCIs are the big ideas of science that provide explanations for a host of phenomena, serve as tools for investigating and exploring more complex phenomena and solving problems, and are the building blocks for future learning within a discipline.[15] CCCs are also big ideas of science, but they transverse disciplines and serve as lenses through which to examine and explore phenomena.[16] PBL also engages learners in SEPs, which consist of the multiple ways in which scientists and engineers explore and understand the natural and the designed world.[17] There are many scientific practices that students may encounter for the first time, as third-graders have often had very little science before this unit.

In ML-PBL, instruction is designed so that the three dimensions work together to support children in making sense of phenomena and solving problems. The integration of the three dimensions of scientific knowledge makes science teaching and learning a knowledge-building enterprise that uses an evidence-based approach to build models to explain the world around us. This knowledge-in-use perspective presents a substantial shift in the teaching of science and one that PBL—an active and student-centered creative approach to learning—promotes. The ML-PBL system brings together the Framework, three-dimensional learning, and PBL as mutually reinforcing structures for supporting teachers and students in sustained deeper learning.

ML-PBL envisions learning as an ongoing developmental process that purposefully builds on students' current understanding and links experiences to enrich understanding and forge more connected ideas over time by constructing ideas from students' prior understandings, intellectual resources from students' families, and cultural and community-based experiences.[18] The purposeful soliciting and valuing of experiences and knowledge that students bring to the classrooms—a key part of ML-PBL—helps promote the practice of shared sensemaking and knowledge-building. Through these experiences, students value science and learn the value of science relevance to their community. ML-PBL not only takes this developmental approach of building on students' prior knowledge and linking experiences, but it also requires students to use reasoning to obtain evidence. This developmental approach guides the growth of students' knowledge towards a more sophisticated and coherent understanding of scientific ideas.

Promoting Social and Emotional Learning

ML-PBL, with its focus on students asking questions, collaborating to make sense of phenomena, and building artifacts, is well-positioned to enable and enhance social and emotional learning (SEL). SEL includes the forming of positive attitudes concerning one's capabilities, the development of positive identity, developing ownership in a project, the management of emotions that support goal achievement, self-reflection, creating and sustaining supportive relationships, and making reasoned decisions.[19] Ownership is seen when students focus on completing a task they recognize as meaningful, willingly invest their efforts on challenging tasks, and acknowledge these tasks as their own. Ownership is fostered when learners are afforded the independence to choose a course of action supported by instructional follow-through after choices are made. In ML-PBL, ownership is enhanced as students take action that contributes to making sense of questions they have asked, solving authentic problems, taking leadership roles in groups, and exploring how what they learn impacts their community. Students demonstrate ownership by taking deep interest in their work and stating that learning science is important to them, desiring to spend more time learning science, and following through on related and complex tasks. These behaviors encourage students to develop a positive identity as a learner.

The ML-PBL environment focuses on students working collaboratively on making sense of phenomena and building artifacts. While collaboration is often emphasized as key to student learning, ML-PBL takes it a step further by providing discourse supports for listening to one another, repeating (with attribution) what others have said, building on others' ideas, and respecting others' contributions. These skills are critical for nurturing positive interactions and relations within student groups and with their teacher.

ML-PBL initiates student self-reflection through tasks where students make "real" decisions regarding the science problem for which they are seeking a solution. For example, when students are creating artifacts, they need to decide if the model they are building responds to the question under exploration and supports the claims they expect to make with evidence. Self-reflection is also needed for participating in academic discourse. ML-PBL lessons guide teachers to prompt students to consider the evidence they have to support a claim and to question one another about the evidence used when evaluating the claims of others.

DESIGN OF AN ML-PBL PROJECT

ML-PBL provides four integrated project-based science units at the third-grade level that build coherently over the school year.[20] Each project links to the next, with performance learning goals building on one another. For example, the scientific practices in each unit—asking questions, data analysis, and constructing explanations—are used in increasingly complex situations across projects. In the first unit, students engage with explanation construction that the teacher scaffolds with prompts, guidance, and questions. By the fourth unit, students use these same practices; however, the teacher's scaffolding is substantially reduced, and students engage in explaining more complex phenomena.

Recognizing the essential importance of the Driving Question in PBL, ML-PBL makes use of these questions across the six weeks of each unit. Throughout the unit, students are prompted to consider the progress they have made in answering the question. At the close of each unit, when students present final artifacts that contain solutions to the Driving Question, the students reveal sustained work in understanding the phenomenon they have learned over the past several weeks.

In ML-PBL, every lesson supports students in developing the science understanding necessary to address the final artifact. Ultimately, through the development of the final artifact, the students answer the Driving Question and meet the grade-level standards described in the Next Generation Science Standards (NGSS). Appendix A presents a description of each unit. Appendix B presents a summary of the third-grade units and shows their Driving Questions, phenomena, and artifacts.

Each unit builds coherently to meet a three-dimensional performance learning goal comprising a scientific practice, a disciplinary core idea, and crosscutting concepts. In the third unit, the Driving Question, *How can we help the birds near our school grow up and thrive?* is answered through the construction of a bird feeder. Initially, students hone their observation skills by searching for birds around the school and asking questions concerning whether the birds they see may—or may not—have the same survival needs. Next, students figure out which environmental resources, such as nuts, berries, or insects, the birds depend on for survival, by searching for and identifying those resources near their school. This is followed by students exploring how birds change their behaviors through the year to meet those needs and why some birds fly south while others remain. The unit ends with the students building a bird feeder that meets the needs of their selected bird and explain why it does so. Appendix B, "Anatomy of an ML-PBL Lesson," provides an overview of the main features of an ML-PBL unit.

PROFESSIONAL LEARNING IN ML-PBL

To support teachers in enacting ML-PBL units, the team provides yearlong professional learning (PL) opportunities. The PL schedule includes a three-day, in-person summer institute that introduces teachers to the four ML-PBL units; here, they participate in small- and whole-group discussions, learning about the use of evidence to support teaching and learning. In these face-to-face PLs, new ML-PBL teachers have the opportunity to engage with teacher leaders who have taught the units in previous years. These experienced ML-PBL teachers serve as mentors and engage in troubleshooting, which results in a robust and collaborative PBL community. Whenever possible, facilitators place ML-PBL first-years in small groups with experienced teachers.

In addition to the in-person sessions, there are biweekly video teacher and team leader check-ins throughout the year. These video conferences have two purposes: they support teachers in using the lesson structure, and they foster community-based support for the challenging ML-PBL practices. The online meetings focus on one of the features of the lesson structure and provide either a backward view (the Learning Set the teachers just completed) and/or a forward view (the Learning Set they are preparing to teach). These collaborative discussions help to build a learning community where teachers can respond to one another around the struggles they may be encountering and can encourage one another in problem solving.

The Design of Professional Learning

The PL framework facilitates sensemaking about lesson design before and after each unit as well as during enactment. Teachers engage in ML-PBL experiences as learners, focusing on key lessons across the unit. The intention is to motivate teachers in sensemaking about the progression of learning in and across the units as well as the value of the Driving Question and the final artifact. The format addresses the features of PBL: it includes a teaching-focused Driving Question (*How can we support students in sensemaking in PBL?*), teacher collaboration, and a PL-focused artifact—a teacher-created model of the progression of student three-dimensional learning in the unit.

Each PL has the following design: (1) the session begins with a Driving Question about the teaching practices of ML-PBL and the NGSS; (2) the teachers immerse themselves in *several lessons across the unit*, considering how learning develops toward the proficiencies needed to construct a final artifact; (3) the teachers create the final artifact of the unit; and (4) the teachers return to the Driving Question of the PL and work as a community to answer their own questions, which were placed on the Driving Question Board.

One aim of the PL is to support teachers' understanding of the lesson structure, which is analogous to the scaffolds provided to students in three-dimensional learning. Three-dimensional instruction represents a major change in teacher practice in their orientation toward science knowledge as encompassing science practices and crosscutting concepts. Instead of positioning the teacher as facilitating the acquisition of facts and concepts, the teachers learn how to support students in doing science and in figuring out how to apply science ideas.

Advancing ideas of equity and supports for social and emotional learning take considerable time to develop. Just as PL inspires a professional learning community for teachers, it serves as a model for developing a parallel classroom community in which students listen to one another, respect each other, incorporate others' ideas in their work, and frequently collaborate with one another. Each of the ML-PBL lessons features student-driven classroom discussions, where the teacher takes the role of prompting further reasoning, asking clarifying questions, and monitoring who speaks when so that more voices are heard. PL sessions, both in-person and virtually, are deliberately orchestrated so that teachers become keenly aware of the importance of ensuring that all students participate in classroom activities and that all voices are heard and respected.

Another important feature of PL is that teachers learn to view the lessons not as scripts but as instantiations of PBL principles that are adaptable and responsive to the students' historical and cultural community. Teachers are encouraged to be responsive to an interest in the community and to be prepared to adapt the lesson in ways that maintain the integrity of PBL principles.

ASSESSMENT DESIGNS IN ML-PBL

At the end of each unit, a post-test assessment is given to all of the students. These assessments are designed using a modified evidence-centered approach.[21] Each assessment and associated rubrics aligns with NGSS performance expectations that require students to use science and engineering practices, disciplinary core ideas, and crosscutting concepts to make sense of phenomena. Although the unit assessments are tied to the NGSS performance expectations, they are not the same phenomena addressed in the units, Driving Questions, or artifacts.

TESTING THE VALUE OF ML-PBL

As a design-based project, the ML-PBL materials were created iteratively over a five-year period. Initially, the team conducted teaching experiments in a small number of classrooms in which classroom observations, videos of enacted lessons, teacher and student interviews, and student artifacts were collected. This process (including the iteration of all instruments and measures) progressed to pilot and field-test studies to ensure that the materials worked as intended to promote student learning, engagement, and community building. During the field tests, post-test and summative assessments were systematically collected, a student social-emotional survey was developed and piloted, and an innovative observative protocol was implemented that measured the degree to which teachers enacted the units with fidelity to the principles of PBL. Finally, an efficacy study was conducted in the fourth year using multiple indicators to examine how students in PBL classes perform when compared with students in classrooms engaged in "business as usual."[22]

The efficacy study focused on determining whether ML-PBL improves science academics and social and emotional learning. In the 2018–2019 school year, a randomized control trial of forty-six midwestern schools (twenty-three treatment and twenty-three control) with 2,371 students was conducted. The treatment consisted of the ML-PBL program, while the control condition received professional development on the NGSS only and continued teaching science with a business-as-usual approach. Pre-test benchmark scores in reading and mathematics were obtained for all sampled students and an independent summative test designed by the Michigan Department of Education was administered. The Michigan summative assessment met the performance expectations in the NGSS and included items that were three-dimensional.

A series of statistical tests showed that the treatment students outperformed the control students, on average, by an eight-percentage-point increase, which meant that a student with only basic skills would become proficient. This percent change is considerably higher than other recent elementary science tests.[23] Moreover, the treatment effect held when accounting for differing reading ability (benchmark), gender, school level, race, ethnicity, and social class as well as regions of the state (which include urban, suburban, and rural areas). Additionally, results from a survey administered at the beginning and the end of the school year measured SEL across three constructs (self-reflection, ownership, and collaboration), which showed a positive ML-PBL treatment effect. Although compelling, these quantitative results do not show how ML-PBL operated in a classroom to obtain these effects. Rich descriptive portrayals of selected elementary teachers offer insight with which to better understand the full impact and nuances of how ML-PBL achieved these effects.

DEVELOPING THE CASE STUDIES

The nine cases presented here represent teachers from the efficacy study and a few from the pilot and field test. The case studies were purposefully selected to present compelling stories that highlight specific features of ML-PBL, how teachers use them, and how the teachers' enactment transforms the classroom into an environment that builds and supports academic and student SEL. They also illustrate the opportunities and challenges teachers faced when enacting ML-PBL. Each case study is richly supported by classroom descriptions and quotes from teachers and students. (At times, the case studies have been edited for readability. Names have also been changed to preserve anonymity.) The cases take you into the classroom as teachers learn to use the principles of PBL and sharpen their practices by continuing to teach ML-PBL. They present narratives from nearly two hundred classroom observations, video analysis of classroom enactments, student and teacher interviews, SEL surveys, student artifacts, pre- and post-tests, and summative assessments.

The first set of four cases details how teachers use the Driving Question, discourse moves, literacy practices, and digital technology to advance science learning. In chapter 2, you meet Mr. Starr, who uses questioning and scientific practices to tie lessons together and pushes students to provide evidence to support their claims. The second case, focusing on veteran teacher Ms. Smith, shows how she learns to use discourse moves to support students in gaining social-emotional competencies. Next is Ms. Lane, in chapter 4, who integrates literacy practices to support students' learning of science. In chapter 5, Ms. Lawson draws on multiple digital tools to enhance learning opportunities and level the playing field for her students, who have a wide range of foundational literacy skills.

The next set of cases includes five cases, the first two of which focus on academic learning in suburban and urban settings. Concentrating on science learning, chapter 6 shows how Ms. Kramer focuses her students on examining phenomena through a systems perspective (a crosscutting concept); while in chapter 7, Ms. Tilson uses a variety of ML-PBL strategies to support her students in academic learning. Ms. Hegg, in chapter 8, demonstrates how ML-PBL science learning is integrated with other subjects, such as mathematics and reading, to promote student learning across the curriculum. Chapter 9 introduces Luzmaria, who demonstrates how the ML-PBL features enable her to connect science phenomena to her bilingual students' cultural experiences, reinforcing culturally relevant pedagogy.[24] Finally, in chapter 10, we meet Ms. Butler, a science educator whose experiences with ML-PBL and the principled professional learning opportunities helped her become a teacher leader in her inner-city district. Altogether, these cases present vivid narratives of teachers and students in their elementary classroom as they engage with ML-PBL. As transformation of practices is not always easy, the cases show how the teachers became more proficient with project-based science learning, using new teaching practices to support students in figuring out phenomena or solving real-world problems.

The final chapter discusses common opportunities and challenges experienced by the teachers in enacting ML-PBL. From the evidence, we provide helpful suggestions for teachers and teacher leaders for reforming science teaching in elementary classrooms so that children can learn to use science ideas and practices to make sense of the world in which they live.

CHAPTER 2

Supporting Students in Figuring Out Phenomena

SELIN AKGUN

Mr. Starr recalls his first days of teaching science with the Multiple Literacies in Project-Based Learning (ML-PBL) program. Having spent more than ten years teaching science using traditional practices, he remembers how anxious he was while changing his mind-set about using different teaching practices and keeping his students engaged. After learning about the new teaching science program through his school administration, Mr. Starr attended several professional learning sessions and decided to step out of his comfort zone. During his first year of teaching science with ML-PBL, he felt the pressure of getting used to new lesson plans, the Driving Question Board, and implementing different pedagogical strategies to support students in figuring out phenomena. Over three years of teaching with ML-PBL, Mr. Starr's anxiety has faded and been replaced with the joy of enacting dynamic science classes.

This case reflects on Mr. Starr's first year experience of teaching third-grade science with ML-PBL practices. His teaching journey illustrates how even an experienced teacher goes through a learning period with ML-PBL. He recalls, "When I taught science before, it was just a mismatch. We kind of touched on things, it was a quick in and out—we covered it, but not in the way it should have covered." However, once he began to learn how to use ML-PBL practices, Mr Starr started seeing a difference in how his students engaged in science learning and making sense of phenomena: "Now my students and I are figuring things out, they are asking questions, and every lesson they do is putting together a piece of knowledge to help them understand what they are learning." This case focuses on how Mr. Starr supports students' sensemaking by using three key principles of ML-PBL: Driving Questions, discourse moves, and multimodal representations.

DRIVING QUESTIONS TO SUPPORT STUDENTS' MAKING SENSE OF PHENOMENA

Within the ML-PBL program, Mr. Starr implemented three distinct third-grade science units in his classroom. Through the Squirrels, Toys, and Birds units, Mr. Starr had the opportunity to cover the overall concepts of survival mechanisms and physical structures of squirrels, magnetic forces and the motion of objects, and similarities and differences in different bird species. While teaching these units, he aimed to elevate students' self-discovery process by making them the active agents of their own knowledge construction process—instead of acting as the authority in his students' learning experience. For example, rather than directly explaining the survival mechanisms and adaptation of different species, Mr. Starr posed a number of Driving Questions about the body structures of squirrels (their teeth, claws, and so on) that help them survive in their habitat. These Driving Questions are one of the distinctive principles of project-based learning (PBL) that help students find the meaning and relevance of a phenomenon and sparks their wonder and curiosity toward science.[1] By using Driving Questions, Mr. Starr put students in an environment in which they could raise and answer questions, make observations, and form claims about scientific phenomena themselves. What is unique about ML-PBL is that, regardless of the specific unit, students all have firsthand experiences where they can make clear connections with the Driving Questions and figure out phenomena in a collaborative and dynamic fashion.

Mr. Starr's Initial Use of the Driving Question

At the beginning of the school year, Mr. Starr started teaching the Squirrels Unit. As a ML-PBL teacher in his first year, he struggled to organize the lesson around the intended Driving Question. However, after practicing using Driving Questions, he improved his teaching in a visible way. For instance, in one of his previous lessons in the Squirrels Unit, Mr. Starr had started the class with the aim of teaching about squirrels' survival in their own habitat. During the class, he did not explicitly use the unit's overall Driving Question: *Why do I see so many squirrels but can't find any stegosauruses?* Instead, he used open-ended, guiding questions like "We talked about how the structures of the squirrel help [her] to survive in an environment with other organisms. What can you tell me about squirrels' structures?" Even though Mr. Starr did not use and revisit the lesson's specific Driving Question, he facilitated discussion by making connections and forming a bridge between the students' prior and current scientific ideas.

A few weeks later, in another lesson from the Squirrels Unit, Mr. Starr begins making more explicit connections with the suggested Driving Question. More excitingly, in one of his final lessons in the Squirrel Unit, Mr. Starr directly highlights and revisits the Driving Question more than once:

> Okay, so what are fossils, and how do they help us understand prehistoric organisms and environments? Lots of big words in that question. We talked about prehistoric. What did we say: "Pre-" means "before," right? So, it is before history—we have to look at structures in order to find out how things happen. So, we looked at some different periods and time. We said we had two different periods: the Ordovician and Silurian periods. That happened 495 million years ago.

Here, Mr. Starr is explicitly raising the Driving Question, *What are fossils and how do they help us understand prehistoric organisms and environments?* and supporting students' literacy and language skills by first unpacking the term "prehistoric organisms."

DISCOURSE MOVES TO SUPPORT THE DRIVING QUESTION AND STUDENTS' SENSEMAKING

Mr. Starr also benefits from *discourse moves* to support and cultivate students' engagement with the Driving Question and to provide an interactive and collaborative learning environment. Discourse moves represent a variety of facilitative strategies, such as helping students to clarify their thinking and deepen their reasoning, making students' ideas public, emphasizing particular scientific ideas, supporting students to listen to others' ideas, and applying their own thinking to others' ideas.[2] These moves allow Mr. Starr to enrich opportunities for students to reason and express their thinking. In addition, as a response to Mr. Starr's discourse moves, students take initiative and participate by using their own moves, like telling and restating ideas, clarifying their thinking, and building on their peers' ideas and comparing and questioning them. Mr. Starr's discourse moves act as an initiator for students to express their own ideas to find their own voices. They not only represent Mr. Starr's teaching and facilitating trajectory, but also show how students take ownership of their ideas, figure out the world around them, and exercise their sense of agency as active learners.

The following example from the Squirrels Unit illustrates Mr. Starr's use of discourse moves and students' participation. Mr. Starr is ready to move the class's previous discussion about earlier forms of organisms a step further. He plans to facilitate a conversation about prior organisms, fossils, and animals' changing environments. He guides students to make claims about how animals might have interacted according to their relative sizes. Before elaborating further on different animals' sizes and features, the class talks about earlier forms of plants. Mr. Starr smoothly makes a connection between the previous and current lesson by using some reminders:

MR. STARR: Two days ago, we talked about how we know about plants from the past. So, what were some ways that we discovered we can learn about the plants from the past? Jonah?

JONAH: You should have evidence.

MR. STARR: Can you tell me more?

JONAH: So, there should be like stones of them, of like the plants, so you know them.

MR. STARR: So, my question was, "How we can talk about plants from a long time ago?" and Jonah said, "By using evidence." I asked him to tell me more and he said, "If they were around, there should be stones of the plants." Who can add more to that or add some details to that? Betty?

In this conversation, Mr. Starr first reminds the students about the Driving Question from the previous class and gives students a chance to refresh their minds regarding the plants from the past. Here, Jonah underlines the importance of using evidence. Mr. Starr's continuous reminders about using evidence help the students understand how scientific phenomena are formed.

After hearing Jonah's response, Mr. Starr asks him to tell more, to clarify his idea. Mr. Starr's clarifying question assists Jonah to dive more deeply into his thoughts. Jonah's follow-up answer about the stones of plants refers to a later form of the plant in its life cycle. For example, thinking about the life cycle of a leaf, it may fall onto the ground, then decay and mix with other earth materials.

Or it may fall into a river, where it sinks into the sand, and a leaf-shaped imprint is formed. In time, the sand slowly hardens into a rock, like sandstone. Millions of years later, someone may pick up the stone and observe the shape of the leaf, which is now a plant fossil. Therefore, Jonah's answer has importance, since it shows his awareness about the previous form of plants, and he can assert this information as a piece of evidence to support his claim.

Following Jonah's answer about stones, Mr. Starr decides to summarize the full conversation from beginning to the end. He revoices the Driving Question to remind students about the core point of the discussion.[3] He restates Jonah's ideas and acknowledges his contribution. In this way, he gives Jonah ownership of his idea and makes his thinking public again. As a final move, he asks if someone can add more to Jonah's ideas. This particular move helps students apply their thinking to others' ideas. It also keeps students alert, because they need to pay attention to their peers' ideas in order to build on them. The rest of the conversation continues with other students' contributing to Mr. Starr's question:

BETTY: In the ground, it would be probably deeper.

MR. STARR: In the ground, it would probably be deeper—how would I have a stone of a plant? Maud?

MAUD: If you leave a plant and have sand for some time, it would be a stone.

MR. STARR: Okay. So you told me that if I left a plant and sand for a long time, the sand would get harder and turn into the stone.

MAUD: Yes.

MR. STARR: So, what's a name for that? Sand or stone?

STUDENTS: Fossils!

Here, Betty's answer enriches the flow of discussion and allows Mr. Starr to raise the question of how plants can turn into stone. Maud adds to Jonah's idea by proposing the role of sand and the effect of time during the formation of the stone plant. Then, Mr. Starr acknowledges Maud's idea and revoices it for others by rephrasing it in a clearer and more meaningful way. Thus, other students easily respond to Mr. Starr's final question and they capture the notion of fossils.

Mr. Starr continues to use discourse moves to guide students to understand the change in plants over a long period of time: "Maud is saying that, and that's what you guys meant. We're talking about fossils, right? So, if we use fossils to talk about plants, how can we look at that and we see the fossils like flowers?"

When the students remain silent, Mr. Starr uses a discourse move: "Let me ask my question again. I know you are confused. Let's use flowers, for example. So, one of them was on our table, right? What can you tell me about the flowers that lived a long time ago? Mary?"

Here, Mr. Starr's initial question does not resonate with students. When he encounters silence from the students, he restates the question by providing a short example from their daily experiences. He uses the word "flowers" as a stepping-stone to help the students make connections about plants. By using the terms "plants" and "flowers" interchangeably and rephrasing his question, Mr. Starr aims to put forward the particular idea of the flower's changing structure. In relation to this question, Mary, Toni, Brad, and other students take part in a good flow of discussion:

MARY: I would look where they are at?

MR. STARR: Why did you say that?

MARY: Because some of them might be still there.

MR. STARR: How many of you agree with Mary? She just said that flowers from long ago are still around. Okay, Toni, why do you raise your hand?

TONI: I disagree with Mary, because I think what happens to the dinosaurs happens to the flowers.

Here, Mr. Starr's guiding question starts the deeper argumentation and discussion environment. While Mary claims the flowers from the past are still around, Toni has a counterargument that previous flowers disappeared like dinosaurs.

In the rest of the discussion, Mr. Starr challenges Toni's ideas about the disappearance of the flowers. Brad also refocuses on different forms of plant fossils and recognizes that their firsthand experiences and videos are the evidence of plant fossils.

MR. STARR: So, we don't have flowers anymore?

TONI: We do.

MR. STARR: But you said what happens to the dinosaurs happens to the flowers. So, we have flowers right now, right? We don't have dinosaurs. But we have fossils of them? So, somebody told me about flowers. Brad?

BRAD: We are talking about flowers.

MR. STARR: Tell me about that. How would you know that they are not here?

BRAD: Because when we watched the video there were no flowers, but fossils.

Through Mr. Starr's guiding questions, Brad and the other students think about each other's ideas by proposing supportive and counterarguments for one another. Instead of directly explaining the scientific phenomena, Mr. Starr uses a variety of discourse moves and guides students to develop their own arguments in relation to the Driving Question of the lesson. These kinds of interactions among students are really what ML-PBL is trying to foster while providing a sensemaking process for students. Even though these third-graders are being exposed to the challenging topic of plant fossils for the first time, they are navigating a fruitful discussion and participating in discussions well.

CONTINUED PROGRESSION ON USING DRIVING QUESTIONS WITH DISCOURSE MOVES—FROM THE SQUIRRELS UNIT TO THE BIRDS UNIT

It is critical to observe how all of the units use the Driving Question with discourse moves to advance students' curiosity about and interest in understanding science phenomena. This is even more evident in the Birds Unit, where we see again how Mr. Starr continually asks open-ended questions related to the Driving Question, revisits them in each lesson, and in the process uses discourse moves to promote students' thoughts about the Driving Question. Most importantly, during the Birds Unit, he does not use the Driving Questions as scripts—instead, he creatively modifies them according to the students' individual and collective knowledge. This allows him to facilitate a more "natural" conversation with his students, rather than a prescribed and artificial discussion. Through modifications of the Driving Question, Mr. Starr reveals students' real-world experiences and observations about the world around them. In this way, students' voices become prominent, inspiring them to engage with new, enduring questions and connect these with their own experiences.

In the Birds Unit, the overall Driving Question for the unit is *How we can help the birds near our school grow up and thrive?* To unpack this Driving Question, Mr. Starr also raises a number of lesson-specific Driving Questions that lead students to answer the overall Driving Question for the unit at the end. With this aim, Mr. Starr creates a discussion environment by asking the following lesson-specific Driving Question: *Are there other traits that are similar and different between birds of different species?* After introducing this question, he also recalls the Driving Question from the previous lesson—*Which traits of female and male cardinals are similar, and which are different?*—in order to promote students' distinctive observations about cardinals, as well as to build on their initial and current ideas toward the Driving Question.

MR. STARR: You looked at cardinals that are male and female and you drew the differences and similarities that you noticed between the male and female cardinal. Can somebody please share with us one of the differences or similarities that you noticed between the male and female cardinal? Sally?

SALLY: The male is bigger than the female.

MR. STARR: Okay, what I heard Sally say was the male is bigger than the female. All right, what's another similarity or difference? Laura?

LAURA: The female is brown, and the male is a vibrant red.

MR. STARR: So, Laura said the female is brown and the male is a vibrant red. How many of you would agree with that? Cameron?

CAMERON: They have an orange beak.

MR. STARR: Okay, they may have an orange beak. Are there any other differences? Okay, let's remember the question again. Are there other traits that are similar and different among male and female cardinals? Who can show and tell me evidence? Abraham?

In the example above, we can see how Mr. Starr uses students' previous observations and experiences to collectively share their ideas by considering the appearance of male and female cardinals. As students express their thoughts, they construct their knowledge together to make sense of the similarities and differences in the same species. After revisiting the previous class through students' explanations on differences between male and female cardinals, Mr. Starr again raises the Driving Question of the lesson, then expands on it by asking for students' observations of the cardinals from the playground:

MR. STARR: Okay, so let's go back to my main question here: "Are there other traits that are similar and different between birds of different species?" Let's say we have a cardinal over here. But what was the first one we saw this morning in the playground?

STUDENTS: A goose!

MR. STARR: This morning, we went out to the playground and we saw a goose and we heard a cardinal. So, let's talk about the goose and cardinal. Are there any similarities between the two?

BRAD: They both have beaks.

WYATT: They both have wings.

MAYA: They both have feet.

GABRIEL: They both fly with their feathers.

AMBER: They both have feathers that help them keep warm.

JAMES: They both eat worms.

MR. STARR: Okay, why do you think they both eat worms? What do you know about these birds?

JAMES: Because I see them outside and in the video.

MR. STARR: Oh! Okay, so now we're bringing in some evidence for backing up our claim. James said, "I know they eat worms, because I've seen the cardinal pecking the ground and I watched the video that says he put worms in his baby's mouth." Now we're bringing evidence into this.

In this conversation, Mr. Starr and his students carry out a rich discussion about the similarities between different bird species—geese and cardinals. Mr. Starr makes students think about their own observations about differences between these particular birds. Providing a real connection and context by using geese and cardinals, he helps the students build their own ideas. Mr. Starr also elicits the significance of using evidence to support claims, as he continuously does here.

MULTIMODAL REPRESENTATIONS TO REINFORCE STUDENTS' SENSEMAKING

In addition to the Driving Questions and discourse moves, Mr. Starr also uses a variety of multimodal representations to support students' sensemaking during his first year enacting ML-PBL. Multimodal representations support students' learning process by integrating the elements of different modalities—such as language, symbols, and depictions—while introducing science ideas.[4] In Mr. Starr's classroom, these multimodal representations take the form of verbal explanations, visuals, analogies, models, texts, videos, and diagrams. Each type of multimodal representation plays a complementary role to support students' figuring out of a phenomenon, as well as to help them see the value of using "evidence" and "claims" in science. Mr. Starr also uses these multimodal texts to support students' mathematical literacy and mathematical thinking in science lessons.

Following are excerpts from the Squirrels Unit and the Toys Unit that reflect students' multimodal experiences. In the Squirrels Unit, the learning goal is to understand squirrels' bodily structures and survival mechanisms in their environments by using mathematical thinking. In the Toys Unit, the learning objective is to develop and support claims about the motion of objects by using magnets. By engaging with these science learning goals through multimodal experiences, students begin to integrate mathematical thinking and evidential claims by measuring, observing, and investigating scientific phenomena.

Mr. Starr's Use of Multimodal Representations in the Squirrels Unit

Mr. Starr heads into class with the lesson's Driving Question in mind: *What are some of the bodily structures of the squirrel that you observe?* He starts a dialogue with the students:

MR. STARR: How does the squirrel eat the acorn?

SALLY: With their front teeth.

MR. STARR: Yes, the front teeth. How do you know that, Sally? What's your evidence?

SALLY: Because when, Mr. Starr, you showed us the video, I saw its arms and its teeth.

MR. STARR: So, Sally's evidence is that the squirrel eats with its sharp teeth and when she [the girl in the video] held the skull, the squirrel had a sharp tooth.

In this dialogue, Mr. Starr first underlines the word "evidence," as he always does in his lessons. Then he uses some visuals and videos of squirrels and marmots to highlight structural differences in their bodies. Since the squirrel family tree includes marmots, Mr. Starr also mentions their bodies to make connections with those of the squirrels: "We were watching a video about marmots before and its tail was moving to help her balance. So, we're going to watch another video of the squirrel today. I want you to pay attention. Then, we will start to talk about marmots and squirrels. Here is the picture of them."

After showing the pictures, Mr. Starr asks: "How is the marmot different from the gray squirrel?" This question starts a rich thread of conversation among students and Mr. Starr:

JAMIE: [The marmot's] bigger.

MR. STARR: Tell me more, please. Let's talk about "bigger"—Jamie said it's bigger. What's "bigger"?

GABRIEL: I think it's the size of an average house cat.

MR. STARR: How do you know that?

GABRIEL: I heard in the video.

MR. STARR: So, you've heard in the video that its size is of an average house cat. What else besides "bigger"?

WYATT: I think it's fatter.

MR. STARR: Describe "fatter" to me. So, you think its body is fatter. Everybody look at that animal. Do you think that the [squirrel's] skinnier than the [marmot]?

STUDENTS: Yes.

MR. STARR: What else do we see here about the marmot?

MAYA: It's taller.

MR. STARR: So, Maya, do you mean its length? What do you think? Is it longer than the squirrel?

MAYA: Yes.

In this conversation, Mr. Starr raises clarifying questions to elaborate students' observations as their evidence. He encourages them to give voice to their ideas. This approach reinforces students' involvement and makes them the active participants in the learning community, where they can share their ideas freely in a supportive and collaborative environment.

Following this round of discussion, Mr. Starr takes things a step further and uses multimodal representations by integrating mathematical concepts in science ideas. To do so, he shows different objects (a book, a ruler, and a water bottle) to compare the heights and weights of the squirrels and marmots (see figure 2.1):

> Okay. I'm going to show you a picture of a marmot. Let me take my markers and ruler. Let's say the marmot weights ten pounds and it is thirty inches long. So, this is thirty inches, right? It is this long. It's like Gabriel's cat's length, right? Let's also say this book is around ten pounds—you can pass the book around to feel how heavy it is. Now, let's take a look at a squirrel . . .

Here, Mr. Starr uses multimodal representations to help students figure out what thirty inches might look like (using the ruler) and what ten pounds might

FIGURE 2.1 Mr. Starr's description of the structure of marmots (using a ruler and a book)

feel (using the book). With these representations, students back up their previous claims and make observations about the appearance and size of the marmot. For instance, after realizing how long thirty inches might be, Gabriel becomes convinced that the marmot's size is quite similar to that of the average house cat. After talking about the marmot's length and weight, Mr. Starr focuses on the squirrel's characteristics: "Okay, let's say the squirrel is about twelve inches long and about one pound. Eastern Gray Squirrels would be about this big [he shows the squirrel picture]. If we compare these ones, the marmot is bigger, right? Also, the squirrel weighs about the same as the water bottle. So, if you hold a water bottle, it weighs about the same as a squirrel. If you compared this water bottle with the book, you could see the major difference."

Again, Mr. Starr uses several multimodal representations to illustrate the real size of the squirrel. In both examples, he integrates mathematical thinking in his explanations. He uses tools (ruler, book, and water bottle) and mathematical units of analysis to show the animals' length (inches) and weight (pounds). In this way, students' abstract ideas become more concrete and they start to compare these animals' physical structures in a better way. These multimodal representations serve as pedagogical tools, which support students' sensemaking.

Mr. Starr's Use of Multimodal Representations and Students' Multimodal Experiences from the Toys Unit

Throughout the Toys Unit, students learn about causal relationships between the motion of objects as well as the strength and direction of magnetic forces. They make investigations to figure out how the distance and movement of the magnetic objects change after magnetic forces are applied. To introduce students to these concepts, Mr. Starr walks around the classroom and poses the Driving Question of the lesson: *How can we change the magnetic forces used to move our toy?* After hearing Mr. Starr's question, students start to revisit their previous ideas and questions about magnetic forces and the motions of the objects. Mr. Starr listens to each answer and encourages students to share their ideas related to the strength and direction of magnetic forces. Following the initial brainstorming about the Driving Question, Mr. Starr explains the next step of their lesson, which is the multimodal investigation of the magnetic forces, and assigns each student to their groups.

In this particular investigation, students work in collaborative groups. Each group investigates a different question. These questions are provided in the investigation chart and concern how the distance, position, and speed of the objects would change with the application of magnetic forces. Students record their observations and measurements in their investigation chart, while Mr. Starr guides them to develop claims by using their measurements as a form of evidence.

While each group is working on their chart, Mr. Starr's research associate, Josh, is also walking around the classroom. Josh approaches Amber, Gabriel, and Nelson's group. They are answering the questions about how the distance between the magnet and paperclip would change with the impact of magnetic forces. Amber and Gabriel place a paperclip on a ruler and place a magnet on one end of the ruler to observe how fast the paper clip moves. Then, Nelson changes the distance between the magnet and the paperclip to see how fast or slow the motion of the paperclip will be. Gabriel and Nelson test the motion of the paperclip for eight different distances, from one-quarter inch to two inches on the ruler. Finally, Amber records their observations on the chart as an evidence of causal relationships between the motion of objects and the strength and direction of magnetic forces.

The students in the group continue testing the motion of the paperclip from different distances and decide whether or not the paperclip has moved toward the magnet:

AMBER: Now, we do one inch.
GABRIEL: Okay, it stuck again.
AMBER: What about two inches?
NELSON: Okay, at two inches, it [the paperclip] doesn't move.

After completing their measurements, they all discuss their observations and Amber reports their findings. In the chart, they define the movement of the paperclip as fast at one-quarter inch, while there was no motion at two inches. Meanwhile, Josh—who has been watching their investigation—engages them in discussion about what they are doing:

JOSH: What are you trying to show here? What's the question? Why are you doing that?
AMBER: Trying to describe what happens with the magnet. If it's going to move or stay or not stay.
GABRIEL: I guess to see if it moves or not. So, non-contact force.
JOSH: Is there a question that you're trying to answer?
AMBER: We're trying to answer how toys are going to move if we add more pressure to our tool to see if it's going to move.
GABRIEL: So, we are trying to build toys for other kids to play with them at home.
JOSH: Okay, thank you.

In this conversation, Josh asks some guiding questions to help students understand the rationale of the investigation. He helps them realize how their observations and notes are essential as a form of evidence to answer the Driving Question. It is important to see how Amber and Gabriel are aware of the multiple aims of their investigations: they realize that they are looking for contact and non-contact forces to observe the motion of the paperclip. While Amber makes a visible connection with the lesson's Driving Question, Gabriel also takes her explanation one step further and reflects on the overall Driving Question for the unit: *How can we design fun moving toys that any kid can build?*

To learn more about the students' approach to the social, cultural, and community aspect of this lesson, we interviewed Mr. Starr. He pointed out that, before this investigation, students watched a short video of a boy in West Africa who made his own toy with the materials he had in his home. He added that this video helped students realize how other students from different parts of the world are also building their own toys with the resources they have on hand. According to Mr. Starr, realizing how other children also delight in building toys on their own helped his students connect and relate to them. As he noted, the joy of creating and playing with toys is shared by children from different societies and cultures around the world.

Additionally, Amber, Gabriel, and Nelson had a chance to interact with several multimodal representations during this investigation. They built a system (model) by using different representations, such as a ruler, paperclip, and magnet, to simulate and figure out how magnetic forces work and how the motion of the magnetic objects would change based on the distance between them. While they were measuring the distances between objects and observing the motion, they also integrated mathematical thinking into their investigation. They placed the paperclip in eight different places on the ruler by measuring the length in inches. Such representation also helps students promote their mathematical literacy while they are trying to make sense of a scientific phenomenon.

DISCUSSION

Mr. Starr's first-year teaching trajectory across three ML-PBL units demonstrates how practical and feasible ML-PBL practices are in supporting students' sensemaking process. First, from the Squirrels Unit to the Birds Unit, Mr. Starr endeavored to connect students' ideas to each other by using Driving Questions, utilizing them to synthesize and summarize what students figured out about a scientific phenomenon. He helped them find the meaning and relevance of the phenomena and sparked their wonderment about the world. Since Mr. Starr's Driving Questions and follow-up guiding questions connected to students' real-world experiences, ideas, and observations, their voices and perspectives became prominent in discussions.

Second, Mr. Starr used discourse moves to cultivate students' engagement with the Driving Question and to provide an interactive and collaborative learning environment. He supported his students to deepen their reasoning, clarify their thinking, and make their ideas public. These moves allowed Mr. Starr to enrich opportunities for the students to reason and express their thinking while figuring out a scientific phenomenon. Mr. Starr's discourse moves acted as an initiator for students to express their own ideas and find their voices. These moves not only represent Mr. Starr's teaching and facilitating trajectory, but also show how students take ownership for their ideas, figure out the world around them, and exercise their sense of agency as active learners.

Finally, Mr. Starr used a variety of multimodal representations—such as videos, diagrams, visuals, and models—to support his students' figuring out process. While doing so, he highlighted the scientific ideas and the importance of claims, evidence, and reasoning multiple times. Multimodal representations acted as tools in his classes to help students address and explore the Driving Question and phenomena. Through experiences and investigations, students formed their own claims and backed up these claims with scientific data from several sources. This exploration process provided a justification for students to link their claims and evidence together and showed them how data can serve as evidence to support their claims.

A 2020 Postscript

Three years later, Mr. Starr remembers his first year of teaching science with ML-PBL: "When I first started to teach with this program, I think I was only using discourse moves in small groups, having students talk to each other and responding to one another. Now, what I am doing is very different." He explains this change by describing the challenges he encountered when first using PBL: "One challenge was obviously the time. It takes a lot of time to set up for stuff, going through the lessons, learning new materials. The other challenge was probably getting kids to think in new ways, like drawing models, asking questions. But the payoff is huge. The payoff is [that] students are figuring out things on their own. Obviously, even after three years, I want to promote my teaching with PBL and students' science ideas."

Although this program challenged Mr. Starr in different ways in his first year, the case above clearly shows how he was actively engaged with different principles of PBL and how he was supporting students' understanding of scientific phenomena even three years ago. Mr. Starr also genuinely thinks that

PBL has changed not only his science teaching, but has also affected his other teaching over the years. Finally, he shares his thoughts on the value of PBL and why it works in his classroom: "What this program gives you is teaching kids how to think and making them question the things around them. I guess it's basically opened up the way I teach, and it gave me a lot more freedom. When students bring ideas, I can circle back around to their ideas, and what I'm doing is making their ideas public. If they feel valued by what you're saying, they're participating more. I think this is one of the biggest takeaways."

CHAPTER 3

Student Social and Emotional Learning in Science

CORY SUSANNE MILLER

The true delight is in the finding out rather than in the knowing.

—ISAAC ASIMOV

It is the middle of the school year in room 314, and Ms. Smith, a twenty-two-year veteran third-grade teacher, reminds her students of the unit Driving Question, How can we help the birds near our school grow up and thrive? Students identify a problem that local birds in their midwestern rural town experience. Ms. Smith asks with enthusiasm, "What are some questions that you have about our big Driving Question? Or what are some questions that you have about solving a problem of the bird that you picked?" She gives the students time to reflect on their ideas and then prompts them to share their questions. Johnny asks, "Why do the bluebirds go away in the winter?" Molly shares that her group wants to know, "How do American robins get the worms in the winter?" Ms. Smith prompts both students to write their questions on a sticky note and place them on the Driving Question Board so they can answer them as they continue learning. Molly and Johnny, both grinning with pride, make their way to the board to display their questions. Even though this is Ms. Smith's first year teaching Multiple Literacies in Project-Based Learning (ML-PBL) and she is inexperienced with using project-based learning (PBL) strategies in her classroom, she is pleasantly surprised by the students' growth in asking meaningful questions and how they have become invested in their own learning.

As PBL emphasizes, when young learners ask questions, investigate, share ideas, and figure out solutions to problems, they see the usefulness of knowledge, build their own understanding of important science ideas, and support their social-emotional development. As the quote by Isaac Asimov suggests, learning is more than just knowing concepts: real learning in science happens during the process of figuring out phenomena. During the figuring-out process, including the practice of asking questions, students are supported in developing self-reflection, ownership, and collaboration skills. Self-reflection requires students to assess their own learning to determine what is important and make decisions to continue developing their knowledge, while also encouraging students to think about how their learning and problem-solving strategies transfer beyond the project to new contexts.[1] Ownership is the feeling of being invested and deeply interested in the work while feeling a sense of belonging, allowing students to tackle challenging problems and take on various leadership roles in their classroom. Finally, collaboration involves students working together to ask questions, investigate phenomena, organize work, regulate their actions, and make sense of the phenomena.

To highlight how PBL supports students' academic learning and the development of their social and emotional learning (SEL), this case details Ms. Smith's third-grade classroom as she teaches the Bird Unit and highlights strategies she learned while participating in the ML-PBL project. This case focuses on the following question: What leverage does using PBL practices provide toward enhancing SEL? As students pursue the Driving Question, the case explores how Ms. Smith engages students in practices including *experiencing and investigating phenomena*, *constructing the Driving Question Board*, and *constructing artifacts* and the role these experiences play in supporting SEL.

EXPERIENCING AND INVESTIGATING PHENOMENA

March is a perfect time for bird-watching as birds return north for the spring. Visiting Ms. Smith's classroom, we see how she excites her students to observe birds together and share what they have noticed about their features, behaviors, and habitats.

Scenario 1: Building relationships to promote collaboration. *Ms. Smith gathers her students on the carpet, welcoming them with a friendly, "Good morning." Once stu-*

dents settle, she continues, "I want to remind you of our Driving Question, How can we help the birds near our school grow up and thrive? *Turn and talk to someone near you about a time you have seen any birds outside. What were they were doing?"*

Ms. Smith asks the students to share, but instead of sharing their own stories, she asks them to share what they heard their partner say. Students share stories about birds they have seen eating, nesting, or flying. Ms. Smith invites the class to gather their science notebooks and their binoculars as they line up at the classroom door with their partner. She then hands out identification cards with pictures of birds that they might see. Before they make their way outside, Ms. Smith asks them to set some common guidelines for their bird-watching adventure. Students remind each other to stay quiet and move slowly so they do not scare away the birds. Bobby cautions his friends, "We should whisper so the birds don't fly away." Ms. Smith shares one final important expectation about sharing binoculars: "If you see a cool bird, you look at it, and then hand it to your partner so they can look at it too."

Ms. Smith supports students in collaborating from the moment they enter her classroom to the moment they leave. In this scenario, she asks her students to turn and talk, and then share with the class what their partner said. This strategy, learned during a ML-PBL professional learning (PL) session, allows students to practice active listening skills by repeating another individual's ideas, a crucial skill for communication and relationship building. Students cannot learn to communicate and build deeper relationships to work collaboratively without first hearing and understanding others' ideas and feelings.[2] Using this strategy allows students to practice listening to others, which can transfer to other discussion opportunities throughout their day—both at school and at home.

As the lesson continues, students head outside to explore the local birds. Being in a quiet, rural community, students have plenty of space to wander with their binoculars. The next scenario follows the students as they look for birds and illustrates how this opportunity to explore phenomena encourages ownership and collaboration.

Scenario 2: Investigating phenomena. *Ms. Smith points out a large brush pile with a few birds sitting on it. As students quietly focus their binoculars, Logan remarks that he thinks the bird is a chickadee. Ms. Smith asks for his evidence: "Why do you say it is a chickadee?" Logan looks at his identification cards and responds, "Well, it has black and white like the picture." The class stops and sits down to write in their* *notebooks. Ms. Smith prompts them to write down their observations—for example, what they hear, what the birds are doing, and where they are. Olivia confirms Logan's observations: "They are black and white with some spots on them!" These casual conversations continue for the twenty minutes while students observe birds.*

After students finish collecting data, they share their observations with a partner. They work together using their identification cards to see if they can identify the birds they observed. Ms. Smith asks students to share their observations with the class. Kate shares that she saw vultures circling the school, and that they were all black. Hannah jumps in to suggest that the bird circling the building was more like a hawk because it was big and had white spots. Allison adds that she saw a bright red cardinal land on a tree branch and then fly to the ground.

Ms. Smith engages her students in phenomena by observing and classifying the birds using their physical features. She asks questions to help students clarify their thinking; for example, asking for evidence from the identification cards, which include science information that describes the features of the birds. These cards draw students' attention to the same features that ornithologists use to classify birds. Providing these tools to students promotes ownership because they experience the authentic work of scientists. These authentic and relevant experiences motivate and influence students to become invested in learning.

Sharing observations and identifying the birds provided another opportunity for students to share their ideas with others, actively listening to and revoicing each other's ideas. During this sharing, Kate and Hannah noticed that they identified the same bird as different species. Kate thought she observed a vulture, but Hannah thought it was a hawk. Interestingly, this conversation between Kate and Hannah convinced Tyler that the question in his mind would be important to ask and place on the Driving Question Board. (Tyler will share his question in the next scenario.) When students collaborate during ML-PBL units, they assist each other in developing questions, conducting investigations, organizing data, and making claims. These multiple opportunities for student collaboration support an active classroom culture that relies on students to drive the figuring out process that leads to making sense of the phenomenon.

Ms. Smith explained that with ML-PBL, her students developed important skills throughout the year as they explore different phenomena, becoming "more inquisitive and more aware and curious of their surroundings." She hopes that these awareness skills will transfer to other areas of their lives, in becoming aware of themselves, others, and their communities.

USING THE DRIVING QUESTION BOARD

Back in room 314, it is evident that Ms. Smith has learned to use the Driving Question Board and to see how her practices changed across the year. The following scenarios illustrate how constructing the Driving Question Board and daily interactions with it promote ownership, self-reflection, and collaboration.

Scenario 3: Developing ownership by asking questions. *Students gather back on the carpet. Ms. Smith asks them to think about their experiences using the identification cards: "Are you wondering anything after we went out and observed some local birds? Do you have any questions, maybe, that will help us answer our Driving Question?" For several minutes, students write their individual questions or wonderings on sticky notes to place on the Driving Question Board. They know they will see the Board each time they come to science and revisit their questions. Logan asks, "How do we help them if they are injured?" Tyler asks, "Why do the red-tailed hawk and the turkey vulture look the same?" Kate asks, "How can we help them if we can't touch them?" Aidan asks, "What would they eat?" Hannah does not have a question, but she wants to help the birds that the hawk might hunt. Ms. Smith helps Hannah to change her statement into the question: "How can I help birds so they don't get eaten by the hawk?" Allie and Nate both suggest that the class should put up bird feeders or birdhouses. Ms. Smith smiles to herself, as she knows that this is the artifact that students will construct throughout the unit. Other students share their questions, and Ms. Smith invites students to place their sticky notes on the Driving Question Board.*

When students perceive a question as unknown and challenging, their curiosity will enhance their motivation to persist in solving the question, and they will find the experience enjoyable.[3] As students place these questions on the Driving Question Board, they develop ownership of that question and feel driven to seek solutions. Granting students an active role in the learning process helps them develop skills, such as setting and attaining goals and establishing independence.[4] As students take ownership of their learning and set goals for themselves, they exhibit and practice self-management skills.[5] In ML-PBL, students determine the path of their learning by using their questions to drive the figuring-out process. They have opportunities to reflect on their prior and current experiences that allow them to make connections and take actions that promote and sustain their learning.

Scenario 4: Revisiting the Driving Question Board daily. *Students enter the classroom, retrieve their science notebooks, and find a seat on the carpet. Ms. Smith draws the students' attention to the Driving Question Board. She asks students to pull a few questions from the Board. After reading the first question, she asks students to turn and talk to a neighbor to decide if the question has been answered. The first question is, "Do birds eat different things?" The students take a moment to think and respond by sharing the research they have done on the birds. Mary reports that her bird, the blue jay, eats seeds, but she also knows—from the chart they have filled out using their observations and text-based research—that the hummingbird drinks sugar water and sap. Together, they come to the conclusion that they have answered this question and they can refer to their chart for the evidence. Ms. Smith shares another question, "Why are sandhill cranes so tall?" Students suggest that they need to continue their learning to find out more. They decide to keep that question on the Driving Question Board. Ms. Smith asks if there are any other questions that students wish to add.*

Ms. Smith places the Driving Question Board in a visible place in the classroom so that students can add their own questions, responses, and artifacts that demonstrate their understanding of the phenomenon. Ms. Smith revisits the board daily to allow students the opportunity to reflect and synthesize their learning to determine whether further investigation is necessary. These reflection practices promote students taking ownership of their learning process and build their understanding of the survival needs of birds. In contrast to the beginning of the unit, during this later phase, there are more questions like, "Will the baby bird look like the parent when it is born?" As students practice asking and answering questions, their reflection helps them learn how to ask appropriate questions for their goals: an important component of learning self-management.[6]

Reflecting on the Driving Question and linking to past learning supports students' reflection about their learning process: what is important to them, how well they are learning, and how they learn from their mistakes.[7] As students revisit the Driving Question Board regularly and practice reflection skills, they become more self-aware and recognize their own emotions and thoughts and the influence these have on their behavior.

Ms. Smith did not always use the Driving Question Board in the ways described in the last two scenarios. In the beginning of the year, she placed the board in the back of the room and did not use it daily. As the year progressed, Ms. Smith learned strategies that allowed her students to do more of the question asking and more synthesizing of various ideas necessary to answer the questions on the board. Ms. Smith describes that her understanding of how to use the Board influenced how her students became more involved in building it:

> [At the beginning of the year], I added their learning [to the Driving Question Board] . . . It would be more of what they were verbalizing, and then I would put it on the board after they left the class. That's how I could start to manage it—I was doing it more . . . [By the end of the year], they're organizing and answering the wonder questions [on the sticky notes]. I like that because then they're starting to think about patterns or grouping things, categorizing things.

Scenario 5: Using the Driving Question Board to model collaboration skills. *Ms. Smith begins by gathering a few questions from the Driving Question Board. She reads the sticky note aloud: "Do all males have darker features and females have lighter?" She then asks the students to think about the answer. Henry suggests that some females are darker than males and gives as an example the fact that female cardinals are darker than males. Ms. Smith uses a discourse move to engage other students: "Does anybody want to add to what he [Henry] just said?" Billy agrees with Henry and provides evidence to support his response; he says, "Female robins are darker than male robins, because the female robin has red and the male robin has orangish." Ms. Smith then calls on Rick: "What do you think about what they've said?" Rick responds, "I'm sorry, but I disagree because that's just one bird, you don't have every bird's information like that." Without prompting from Ms. Smith, Billy reminds Rick about the second piece of evidence: "But what about the cardinals [since female cardinals are also darker than the males]?" Ms. Smith revoices Rick's answer: "Rick, what I understand you saying is that it depends on the species?" Rick says, "Yes, it's like half and half [that males are darker than females]." Ms. Smith responds, "So, do you all agree that females and males do look different?" The boys agree that often the female bird looks different from the male bird of the same species, although they cannot conclude that there is a generalized difference of one being darker or lighter. The sticky note is then put back on the Driving Question Board so they can revisit it.*

This conversation demonstrates Ms. Smith facilitating a discussion and modeling questioning strategies. During the discussion, the classmates had different ideas and shared their thinking. Ms. Smith believes that discussions are an important component of ML-PBL. She shares, "It is so important for students to have opportunities to hear their classmates' ideas because it either allows them to solidify their own ideas or think of different perspectives and think outside the box." She noticed that students were becoming more confident and excited about arguing their claims with evidence. Ms. Smith believes these discussion skills are important for building friendships and solving conflicts within relationships outside of school.

Later in this lesson, she asked students to write about whether sibling birds would look the same. As Ms. Smith usually does, she has students share their ideas with a partner. Logan and Chase shared together:

LOGAN: They'll be different, because if one is a boy it will have different colors of fur and girls will have an orange color.

CHASE: I think they would not be the same every time because males and females don't look the same in pictures. And then I was going to say because the colors are different.

LOGAN: Okay. Cool. So, you agree with me?

CHASE: Yes, we both agree.

By modeling discussions, Ms. Smith positioned her students for later collaborative experiences. Both Chase and Logan fully participate in the conversation because that time was "intentionally crafted." Randy and Barrett also had a positive exchange:

BARRETT: I think they're going to grow up and be different from each other. I think that because everybody's different in their own way.

RANDY: No, the bird could be born and get bigger or it could be born and eat less.

BARRETT: I don't get it.

RANDY: But we have basically the same answer.

BARRETT: So, you're basically saying that they're going to be different? They are going to grow and be different from each other?

RANDY: Yes, they could just eat more, and one could eat less.

This excerpt highlights students using the revoicing discourse move that Ms. Smith modeled while they revisited the Driving Question Board. Barrett did not understand his partner, but revoiced what he heard, just as Ms. Smith had done, and it prompted Randy to clarify his response.

Ms. Smith has seen her students grow in their discussion skills—an important aspect of collaboration—over the course of the year. At the beginning of the year, many students did not share their ideas, and she spent time modeling discussions and using discourse moves to scaffold productive communication among them. As the year progressed, students began to use the same discourse moves themselves and learned how to come to agreement. She noticed that they became confident with regards to participating in discussions and ask questions. These skills helped students collaborate to construct the unit artifacts and will support them to work with peers in the future. Ms. Smith shares: "In real life, they're going to be problem-solving [whether or not] they're out in the playground. They're going to be trying to figure out solutions to problems or things that they have going on. I feel like this [ML-PBL] helps them to have the tools to be able to rationalize it and be able to come up with some ideas that make sense or that are realistic and not just . . . run to an adult."

Throughout the school year, Ms. Smith noticed her own growth in using discourse moves. At the beginning of the year, she found herself mostly using them only to repeat student ideas and emphasize ideas, but then became more successful in prompting students to think deeper and compare their thinking to others' ideas. She believes that she was aware of the discourse moves that ML-PBL shared in the PL session but never used them effectively. Experiencing the discourse moves modeled during PL helped to convince her of their value. She shares, "The questioning really pushes them to think deeper—I think they are thinking deeper than they have in the past." She believes that students need to practice providing their own answers and solutions during science instruction so they can use those same skills in other contexts.

CONSTRUCTING ARTIFACTS

As students revisit their questions, they move closer to answering the Driving Question that allows them to take action to solve a real-world problem that encourages their ownership of the question. Students have answered several questions like, "What do birds eat?" and "Which birds stay here in the winter and which ones migrate?" and are now challenged with working with their team to design and build a bird feeder based on their research. Joining Ms. Smith's class, we see how constructing artifacts enhances collaboration skills and supports student self-reflection and ownership.

Scenario 6: Brainstorming solutions to problems. *Ms. Smith prompts students to reflect on previous discussions: "Turn and talk to your partner about some of the problems birds would have related to food that we identified." After a short discussion, she asks for a few responses. Claire shares about her bird, the bluebird, "We looked at the food, and it looks like it eats insects, but the bluebird can't get to the insects all year long." Tommy suggests that hummingbirds have the same problem: "The hummingbird eats nectar, and they cannot get it all year long either." Ms. Smith asks, "But why is that?" Tommy explains, "The flowers might not be out." Ms. Smith follows up by asking for the evidence he has to help clarify his thinking. Tommy adds, "We went out and checked and didn't see any flowers this time of year." Wesson also shares that his bird, the American robin, "can't dig in the ground in the winter [to get food] because the ground is hard." Ms. Smith collects these problem statements as students talk and writes them on sentence strips to display. She shares with the students that their job is to pick one of the problems and figure out a solution. In a short discussion, Ms. Smith asks for ideas about how they might solve the problem, and students suggest that they could build bird feeders. She is prepared with a few examples of feeders to show them, which are made out of recycled materials: milk jugs, soda bottles, juice cartons, wooden spoons, and other materials. She sends students off to work at their tables with their groups.*

In one group, students spend the first few minutes deciding which bird to help. At first, they think about the hummingbird, and decide they would need flowers, sugar water, and a water bottle. The conversation turns as they become discouraged with their choice—building a feeder for a hummingbird seems too difficult. They switch their focus to the American robin. The group uses their research chart to find out what the robin eats, and they decide they need worms and berries in their design. In their discussion, they realize that none of them have a milk jug at home, so they decide to use two cardboard boxes: one with berries, and one with worms. Jack says, "We will have to separate them, because the worms will make the blueberries slimy." They also decide they need sticks for the birds to stand on to get to the food. As the group work time ends, the group realizes they did not have time to draw their design, but they decide that Jenny has the right size boxes, and she will bring them to class tomorrow.

Ms. Smith may not have agreed with the group's plan, but she made sure that students had the opportunity to figure out on their own if it was going to work. The first photo in image 3.1 shows the group's bird feeder after some design changes. She allowed them to build their bird feeder without influencing their decisions, giving them ownership of their work. Ms. Smith shared later that this group experienced a problem when they tested their feeder, due to a record amount of rainfall in the Midwest: "We went out to look at them and they bring back a shredded piece of cardboard and they're like, 'This just isn't a good idea . . . We need to use something with plastic.'"

The students redesigned their bird feeder and were more successful after their revision. This revision process is important in developing self-directed learners. They must critique their work and consider feedback from others to make improvements. Ms. Smith describes what she sees in the revision process: "[They are] coming up with ideas and able to revise their ideas and knowing that some things are going to work but some things aren't. But they are excited that even if it doesn't work, they can go back to it and try to fix it or change it. [They are learning] that it's not always your final thing, and it might be sloppy in the end, and that is okay."

Ms. Smith shares that another group had an elaborate model drawn as their plan for their bird feeder: "They were going to use a milk jug and attach troughs on the bottom and then cut holes for the birds to reach the food. When it came

FIGURE 3.1 Examples of final artifacts built for the Bird Unit

(1) (2) (3)

time to build the feeder, the group realized that their holes were too high, and the birds could not reach the food." Instead of being upset about their mistake, the group adjusted and made the decision to cut the top of the feeder and see how that worked.

A final group of students built a combination of a feeder and a nest for their bird (see examples in figure 3.1). Students need opportunities to make connections and summarize their learning to make future decisions. During the revision process in repairing their bird feeder, students became responsible for their own learning and had to fix mistakes they made to succeed the second time. The ML-PBL experience influences student ownership because students persevere through challenges to achieve their personal goals. These final artifacts exhibit the science knowledge students developed throughout the unit as they needed to take into account the physical and behavioral traits of their focal bird, the changing weather, the features of the environment, and the birds' needs for reproduction.

DISCUSSION

This case explored how Ms. Smith used the practices of PBL to support the development of SEL, including collaboration, self-reflection, and ownership. During this Bird Unit, students pursued the answer to the unit Driving Question, *"How can we help the birds near our school grow up and thrive?"* Ms. Smith engaged students in PBL practices including *investigating phenomena*, constructing and using *the Driving Question Board*, and *building artifacts*. Through classroom observations, field notes, and teacher interviews, evidence suggests that engaging students in these practices can enhance the students' social-emotional development. In the beginning of the unit, students explored phenomena and asked questions that provided motivation for them to develop a sense of ownership of their learning. As students worked together to organize and develop their ideas, they developed communication and relationship skills important for collaboration. Finally, students spent time reflecting on their work to make connections and revise their final artifacts to answer the unit Driving Question. Further evidence supporting this finding is the analysis of students' self-report on an SEL survey given in the fall and the spring. In Ms. Smith's classroom, there were positive changes in students' responses from the beginning of the year to the end in three areas: self-reflection, ownership, and collaboration.

Ms. Smith's development over the course of the year also helps to explain these results. Ms. Smith learned that her students are capable of figuring out phenomena and the value in letting them do so. She learned over the course of the year that if she just gives them the time they need to reflect and figure it out, they eventually will. She shares that the strategies learned from the ML-PBL curriculum and professional learning have allowed her to become a teacher who supports her students in taking some of the leadership in the classroom and making decisions about their own learning. She has also come to realize that if they do not know all of the science content in third grade, that is okay, and that they have learned other skills that are valuable, like problem-solving. Ms. Smith describes her shift in teaching:

> I think before I gave them too much and I felt like it made them a little bit lazy in their thinking and their coming up with the ideas. They were just waiting for me to reveal it to them or give it to them instead of them having to do all the hard work of coming up with it. I have used more wait time—I felt like before I was rushed, so I would, if they didn't give [the answer] to me instantly, it was like, "All right, you just got to give it to them because I can't keep waiting." But I feel like I have seen that when I wait, the kids come up with it.

The practices described in the chapter highlight the possibilities for teachers to integrate SEL into classroom instruction. SEL cannot be taught in isolation but can be taught in the context of students finding solutions to questions they ask about their world. When teachers become effective in the use of PBL features, they provide a classroom environment that allows students to be better equipped to use social and emotional skills and take part in their own self-development.

CHAPTER 4

Creating Opportunities for Students to Use Multiple Literacies

MIRANDA S. FITZGERALD AND
ANNEMARIE SULLIVAN PALINCSAR

> There are embedded and authentic opportunities for students to engage in all aspects of the multiple literacies. This allows students with varying abilities to engage, explain, learn from, and demonstrate their learning and understanding of concepts.
>
> —MS. LANE

Ms. Lane, a third-grade teacher, is keenly aware of her obligation to teach foundational literacy skills (reading, writing, speaking, and listening), in addition to the other subject-matter content for which she is responsible. Participating in the Multiple Literacies in Project-Based Learning (ML-PBL) project over four years, she explains that "there has been this conversation in education about you've got to push math, you've got to push reading. If you have to let science and social studies go to the wayside a little bit, that's okay. Then, it's . . . come back and it's like, "Whoa, no, you can't do that!'" This is a challenge shared by all elementary-grade teachers that has intrigued both language literacy and science education researchers.[1] This case provides glimpses of what instruction at the intersection of language literacy and science literacy looks like in a third-grade classroom engaged in ML-PBL, where the curriculum takes advantage of the synergies between teaching literacy and science.

Ms. Lane teaches at Slate Elementary School, a Title 1 school in a rural district in the Midwest that serves 550 students, of whom 65 percent qualify for free or reduced-price lunch, 20 percent receive special education services, and 5 percent are English learners. Sixty-five percent of the students are white, 25 percent are Black, 5 percent are Hispanic/Latinx, 5 percent are two or more races; only 20 percent of the students in the school are proficient in English language arts.

Ms. Lane is one of the original group of teachers who first piloted the ML-PBL curriculum in the 2015–2016 school year. Drawing on interviews, surveys, and observations during her four years of teaching ML-PBL, this case examines the design and teaching of one text from the Toy Unit, "From Water Squirter to Super Soaker: How Lonnie George Johnson Changed Water Games." This is a biographical text about Dr. Lonnie Johnson, who invented the popular Super Soaker toy. We show how Ms. Lane and her students use the text in the classroom. In the lesson, students predict patterns of motion for different water squirters (including the Super Soaker) before reading about Dr. Johnson and how he applied scientific ideas to develop a design solution. We also illustrate how Ms. Lane and her students connect this text to other tasks and literacy resources in the unit.

FROM WATER SQUIRTER TO SUPER SOAKER

"From Water Squirter to Super Soaker" begins by describing how Dr. Lonnie Johnson addressed a problem with early toy water squirters: that is, they did not get anyone very wet and were not especially exciting to play with. It describes how Dr. Johnson designed the Super Soaker, beginning with his childhood interest in figuring out how things work and inventing at an early age. The text then describes how he studied engineering at Tuskegee University and eventually worked as an engineer for NASA. Finally, it describes the series of events that led to his iterative design and production of the Super Soaker.

The text is accompanied by a reading guide designed to support teacher enactment and to engage students in reading, interpreting, and discussing the ideas presented. Specifically, the guide includes suggested discussion questions, opportunities to engage students in firsthand observations and demonstrations before and during reading, and supplemental information to support building background knowledge about Dr. Johnson and the Super Soaker.

As is the case with many of the texts we include in ML-PBL, the Super Soaker text was read aloud by Ms. Lane, who engaged the class in discussing the ideas in the text as they read. The goals of the discussion included making sense of the ideas in the text, connecting them with the students' firsthand investigations, and connecting them with language and concepts to which students were introduced in the unit (e.g., engineering design, forces, and interactions).

THE FOCAL LESSON

After introducing the unit Driving Question (*How can we design fun moving toys that any kid can build?*), Ms. Lane begins the Toys Unit by engaging her students in making observations and generating questions for the Driving Question Board about commercially produced toys. While investigating toy air rockets, students share their observations and wonderings. For example, Aiden shares, "I noticed that the blue thingy looks like a pump. You probably pump it and the rocket shoots out." Curtis adds to Aiden's thinking: "When you push the blue pump, it sends air through the pipe—the hose—and it goes into the rocket." Ellie wonders what the metal part on the rocket is for, and Julie wonders how far the rocket goes. After observing and asking questions about several moving toys and investigating causes of motion (e.g., push or pull) with a partner, students select a toy from a set of options (milk carton car, skimmer boat, or water-bottle rocket) and build simple prototypes of the toys using written and video instructions. Partners then test their toys' motion and observe how the toys start to move. Students use their observations to develop models explaining the forces that cause their toys to move.

Next, Ms. Lane asks students to brainstorm why other children might want or need to build their own toys and ways the class can design features of moving toys that other children enjoy. As a class, students generate interview questions to ask younger children to gather feedback to improve their prototypes. They conduct the interviews with kindergarteners, debrief the feedback as a class, and plan to make one of the suggested changes to improve their designs. In the next lesson, Ms. Lane introduces the text, "From Water Squirter to Super Soaker."

BUILDING EXPERIENCE AND BACKGROUND KNOWLEDGE

Ms. Lane invites students to gather on the carpet in the front of the classroom; presents three different water squirters, including the Super Soaker; and asks students to observe and describe what they notice about each one. Ms. Lane asks, "Which one do you think may squirt the farthest?" and invites students to vote via raised hands. There is overwhelming consensus among the class that the Super Soaker will shoot water the farthest. Ms. Lane then reminds students of the unit Driving Question and presses for them to share the reasoning behind their votes. "Let me ask you this," Ms. Lane probes, "Because we are talking about engineering and we are talking about making toys that other kids can build . . . why might this [Super Soaker] be the most [successful]? Why might more people think this?"

Two students, Jenna and Julia, point out the sticker on the Super Soaker that says it shoots water over forty feet. Ms. Lane confirms, "So the stickers are . . . telling you it might shoot far." Kayla adds that she voted for the Super Soaker because it's "the longest one, and if it's longer, it might absorb more water." Ms. Lane continues to invite students to make observations and to think about how the parts of each toy system work together.

Ms. Lane next has students test their predictions about which water squirter will shoot the farthest. While the written curriculum proposes that students only briefly make and share observations of the three water squirters (during a ten-minute introduction to the lesson), Ms. Lane chooses to dedicate a full day of science instruction (forty-five minutes) to observing and investigating these toys to extend students' opportunities to identify different parts of the toys' systems, figure out how those parts work together, and make connections to the toys they are designing, testing, and revising. These opportunities allow students to build shared knowledge and experiences regarding the design and function of the water squirters prior to reading about how Dr. Johnson designed the Super Soaker.

In the end-of-unit interview with Ms. Lane, she emphasized the importance of engaging students in firsthand experiences before reading: "I think having the actual Super Soakers visually there and doing the demonstration . . . made the book that much more interesting . . . I think anytime they can see that [in] real life and then see it in a book just magnifies that . . . it's not just words on a page . . . There's meaning there, there's a story there, [and] there's something to learn from it." Ms. Lane highlighted the value of connecting the text to students' firsthand experiences observing and testing the water squirters. This also set up the design problem introduced in the text: Dr. Johnson recognized that while water squirters were fun to play with, they did not get people very wet. Each of these ideas links directly to important goals of the lesson, in which students predict patterns of motion for different water squirters, including the Super Soaker, and use information from the text to identify both the design problem and how Dr. Johnson applied scientific ideas to develop a solution.

CONNECTING TO STUDENTS' KNOWLEDGE AND EXPERIENCES

Before Reading

Before reading the text, Ms. Lane asks students to "[t]hink about anything we've done . . . that might have something to do with this [text] that we're about to read." Cameron quickly makes the connection: "We shot some of those! We shot the Super Soakers . . . outside the cafeteria." "Okay, and what were we hoping to find out?" Ms. Lane asks. "How far they go," Cameron responds. Ms. Lane summarizes: "Okay, how far they would go . . . We looked at three different ones . . . We made observations, we thought about how they might work, and then we went outside and tested them."

In this exchange, Ms. Lane prompts students to recall their shared experience observing and testing the water squirters on the first day of the lesson. To prepare students to read, Ms. Lane summarizes the activity from the previous day, when students tested the water squirters and Super Soaker outside.

During Reading

Ms. Lane also supports students to make connections to their firsthand experiences, such as building their own toy prototypes or models, during reading. For example, while reading the part of the text that describes Dr. Johnson's prototype of the Super Soaker, Ms. Lane pauses the interactive read-aloud (a teacher read-aloud in which the teacher and students are actively engaged in talking about and making sense of ideas in the text): "Think about your toys. They're kind of like prototypes, which is a first model." While this comment does not lead to an extended exchange among students, it illustrates one way in which Ms. Lane prompts students to make connections between the ideas in the text and their firsthand experiences designing their own moving toys.

When the text describes how Dr. Johnson used compressed air to make many of the toys that he designed move, Ms. Lane supports students to make a conceptual connection between the design of the Super Soaker and other toys Dr. Johnson designed. She asks: "What was . . . something that he [Dr. Johnson] found interesting that he kind of used with his robot? He used it with his robot to get his robot to move." One student, leveraging a disciplinary core idea of the ML-PBL unit, suggests that Dr. Johnson used force to make his robot move. Another student, Ellie, clarifies that Dr. Johnson used "compressed air." Ms. Lane repeats this idea and asks students to connect to the Super Soaker: "Compressed air. Think about what we did on Friday. Do you think we were using any compressed air on Friday [when we tested the Super Soaker]?" "Yeah, loads of it!" Lucas replies.

In this example, Ms. Lane pauses during reading to pose a question about an idea in the text. She then prompts students to reflect on their own experiences using compressed air as they investigated the Super Soaker. The students' exchanges with one another and Ms. Lane about compressed air illustrate how they are both drawing on and building their understanding about disciplinary core ideas related to forces and interactions in how Dr. Johnson used compressed air as a force in his design of the Super Soakers students explored firsthand.

After Reading

In the text, Dr. Johnson identified a problem with toy water squirters (i.e., they did not squirt water very far and did not get people very wet), came up with ideas for possible solutions (i.e., using compressed air to increase the force applied and designing a larger chamber to hold water than was typical of other water squirters), and tested and received feedback on his solution by having his six-year-old daughter try out his Super Soaker prototype.

After reading, Ms. Lane invites students to share the engineering practices in which Dr. Johnson engaged. After a few students share their ideas, Ellie adds: "I have something . . . Communicate . . . Like get feedback." Ms. Lane asks Ellie to clarify: "Communicate. And you're saying that's kind of like feedback?" "Yeah," Ellie responds. Ms. Lane uses this opportunity to ask the class to connect to their firsthand experiences during the unit: "When she says communicate and feedback, does that make you think anything? . . . Have *we* done any kind of communicating or feedback?" Students respond affirmatively and share that they communicated and received feedback when they presented their prototypes to kindergartners and asked for feedback about how to improve their toys.

Recall that the class worked together to develop interview questions to gather feedback from kindergartners. These activities—in which students developed, practiced, and conducted interviews—illustrate ways in which multiple literacies were used together in the unit to advance student learning. While discussing the engineering practices in which Dr. Johnson engaged while designing the Super Soaker, students make connections to their experiences eliciting and incorporating feedback from kindergartners.

Linking students' reading to earlier unit experiences and reflecting on and applying the engineering design practices illustrated in the text to improve students' toy designs created a seamlessness between students' reading and first-hand experiences. This supported students to build knowledge about science and engineering disciplinary core ideas (e.g., force and motion) and practices (e.g., testing design solutions), to reflect on their experiences engaging in science and engineering practices, and to connect their reading to the work they would do later in the unit. This echoes Purcell-Gates, Duke, and Martineau's findings that opportunities for elementary-grade students to engage in meaningful reading experiences in the context of science instruction were associated with greater comprehension gains than were more traditional school-based literacy activities, such as reading disconnected texts and reading without using the information in a meaningful way or in the context of meaningful activities.[2]

READING STRATEGICALLY

Ms. Lane supports students to engage in strategic reading during the interactive read-aloud. For example, she engages students in making predictions both prior to and during reading and models how to make connections. Furthermore, she prompts students to make connections to their own experiences and other texts as they read "From Water Squirter to Super Soaker." Ms. Lane pauses frequently during the interactive read-aloud to ask students to relate ideas in the text to their own thoughts, feelings, and experiences. Before Ms. Lane begins reading the text aloud with the class, she asks them to make predictions, based on the title:

MS. LANE: So, "From Water Squirter to Super Soaker." Why do you think it goes from squirter to Super Soaker? Any predictions on that? Aiden?

AIDEN: Because he made a water gun that could wet somebody pretty bad.

MS. LANE: Okay, so which would you want to play with—a squirter or a Super Soaker?

CURTIS: Super Soaker, obviously!

MS. LANE: Okay, you say "obviously." Why would you rather play with a Super Soaker "obviously"? Lucas?

LUCAS: Because it would soak you down and cool you off.

MS. LANE: Right, just the word "soak," you know that you're probably going to drench somebody.

Here, Ms. Lane asks students to make predictions about the text based on the title, "From Water Squirter to Super Soaker." Aiden shares his prediction about what the title might mean, and then the class continues to discuss what the words in the title (i.e., soak) suggest about what they might learn as they read.

After students make predictions, Ms. Lane begins the interactive read-aloud, pausing reading to model how to make connections to relevant prior knowledge and experiences while reading:

MS. LANE: Not that long ago, right? I was alive then [in 1991] "*. . . when the Super Soaker went on sale. With the Super Soaker, you could drench someone with a single blast of water.*" And I will tell you, when we used to do canoes like up and down the rivers with friends, everybody wanted to make sure they had a Super Soaker.

STUDENTS: Why?

MS. LANE: Because if not, *oh*, they were going to get soaked and they had no retaliation . . . So, I'm just making that connection. Whenever you're reading, it's always a good idea, if it makes you think of something else, just kind of say that to yourself.

Ms. Lane pauses as she reads aloud and models making connections to relevant prior knowledge and experiences through a think-aloud. She shares a brief anecdote about her own experiences playing with Super Soakers when she was young and then explains that it can be useful to make connections like this while reading.

This is one of many examples of connections Ms. Lane models and supports students to make during the interactive read-aloud. Supporting learners to make these connections is consistent with the literature emphasizing the importance of making connections to one's own experience, prior knowledge, and related ideas in the service of understanding and remembering.[3]

NOTICING AND USING SCIENCE AND ENGINEERING PRACTICES

Ms. Lane believes the text supported students to notice and deepen their understanding of engineering practices. She shares that, in the text, "There was a question, there was something to ask, [Dr. Johnson] had to come up with a plan, he wanted to create something or the design . . . Seeing it as someone who took it and did something with it . . . an engineer designed this." After reading the text and viewing a short video clip to learn more about Dr. Johnson, the lesson plan suggests that the teacher engage students in a discussion about Dr. Johnson's work as an engineer and identify how Dr. Johnson engaged in engineering design practices such as identifying a problem with toy water squirters, coming up with ideas for possible solutions, and testing his solution by having his six-year-old daughter try out his Super Soaker prototype.

Ms. Lane provides her students with opportunities, both during and after reading and viewing, to discuss engineering practices and to make connections to their own work, in which students designed, tested, and improved their own moving toys. The following example illustrates how Ms. Lane supports students to make connections between the reading and their firsthand experiences designing and improving their own toys.

MS. LANE: How can we tie this into . . . what we're doing in science? What's our Driving Question?

ELLIE: How can we design inexpensive or fun moving toys that other kids can create?

MS. LANE: Okay, so what's that part of in science? Okay, creating. What else?

ELLIE: Engineering.

STUDENT: Lonnie Johnson, he created something with just parts that he found.

MS. LANE: Okay, so kind of scrap parts. Alright. [*Ms. Lane records students' ideas on the whiteboard.*] I heard you say something, Ellie. What did you say?

ELLIE: The engineering design process.

MS. LANE: Okay, so the engineering design process. What do you know about the engineering design process? Think about where we're at in the engineering design process with our toys.

STUDENT: Improve.

MS. LANE: We're kind of making the improvements and going back to plan, right? I think the last thing . . . you guys did was you started to draw what you would do, how you would make your new toy with one of the changes.

On the third day of the lesson, Ms. Lane asks students to connect their learning about how Dr. Johnson designed the Super Soaker to what they were doing in the unit to answer the Driving Question (*How can we design fun moving toys that any kid can build?*). This is an opportunity for students to connect to their own experiences designing and improving their moving toys and also continue their conversation about typical engineering practices (for example, iterative design) as they design, test, and revise their own designs.

In an interview focused on the ML-PBL literacy resources she used during her fourth year teaching the curriculum, Ms. Lane shared how the texts support students to make connections to their firsthand experiences. She explained that the text "pertains to what we're doing, so that they can make those connections. It always seems like there's a reading piece that comes in . . . tying things together, to get them to think about what they've learned . . . Whatever we were reading about, it was not difficult to connect back to that Driving Question." In the Toys Unit, supporting students to make connections to the Driving Question and between what they noticed about Dr. Johnson's use of engineering practices and their own firsthand experiences set the stage for students to continue exploring how different forces affected the motion of their toys; revisit the feedback they received from the kindergarten students; and make new changes to their toys and test how those changes affected their toys' motion in upcoming lessons.

USING SCIENCE LANGUAGE

The use of text in science instruction can provide opportunities to introduce, clarify, use, and reinforce vocabulary, particularly general academic and discipline-specific words that are important for building and communicating disciplinary knowledge.[4] Before and during reading, Ms. Lane leverages opportunities to reinforce, introduce, clarify, and engage students in using general academic (e.g., system) and discipline-specific words (e.g., force).

In some cases, Ms. Lane uses background knowledge-building activities (e.g., observing and testing water squirters) to revisit and reinforce important vocabulary and disciplinary core ideas from the unit of instruction (e.g., force). At other times, Ms. Lane draws on suggestions from the interactive teaching guide to discuss and clarify vocabulary introduced within the text (e.g., compressed air) that is important for building knowledge. Finally, some students ask about the meaning of particular words that are important to understanding the text (e.g., transmitter) as they read.

Before Reading

As students gather on the carpet on the first day of the lesson, recall that Ms. Lane invites them to make observations of the different water squirters. As students share their observations, Ms. Lane prompts them to use the science language to which they were introduced earlier in the unit (e.g., pull, force). Aiden begins by sharing how he thinks the parts of the Super Soaker work:

MS. LANE: What did you say?
AIDEN: If you pull the yellow part [of the water squirter].
MS. LANE: What did you say?
AIDEN: If you use a force to pull the yellow part back.
MS. LANE: You could have just kept saying "pull," but it's great that you made that connection.

Here, while observing the water squirters and Super Soaker, Aiden describes how the parts of the system work together. Ms. Lane challenges Aiden to use science vocabulary (i.e., force) that the class is learning in the unit. After Ms. Lane presses ("What did you say?"), Aiden clarifies that when you pull the yellow part (i.e., pump) of the water squirter, you are applying a "force."

As the conversation continues, Cameron observes that all of the water squirters "suck up and use water" and continues using the word "force" while sharing his ideas:

MS. LANE: So, they suck up and use water. Anything else? Cameron?
CAMERON: You use a force to pull it back under the water and then use another force to push it back so that the water comes out.
MS. LANE: Okay, so on all of them there's a force used to pull up—did you say "water"?
CAMERON: Yeah.
MS. LANE: Or pull in water and then spray it out.
CAMERON: Spray it out.
MS. LANE: So, we'll kind of put "all" here [in the observation notes written on the chart paper]. Anything else you may notice about all of them?

ELLIE: You have to pull something. For each of them, you have to pull something or use a force.

As students continue to make and share their observations of the water squirters, others take up the opportunity to use the word "force" as well.

During Reading

From the text, students learn that Dr. Johnson began using compressed air to make some of the toys he designed (e.g., a robot, the Super Soaker) move. While reading, Ms. Lane and her students pause to discuss this idea on multiple occasions. In one instance, Ms. Lane reads from the text: "When air is compressed, it is pushed into a much smaller space. When the air is released, it pushes back. Lonnie figured out how to use this force to make the robot move." She pauses to ask, "What do you think 'compressed' means? Can you show me what 'compressed' means?" One student, Jessica, clasps her hands tightly together in a ball and squeezes, as other students follow. Ellie holds her hands up in front of her face, spreads her fingers, and pushes her hands toward one another as though she is tightly squeezing a ball. Aiden, and many other students, make their hands flat and press their palms together. Scanning the room, Ms. Lane concludes, "Clearly, I'm not telling you anything you don't already know." She then continues reading aloud before pausing again to revisit the idea:

MS. LANE: We talked a little bit about that compressed air. That's really kind of important. Can anybody give an example of how we can show compressed air? Kaylee? Cameron? Okay, think about a balloon.

STUDENT: It's like a rocket.

MS. LANE: Think about a balloon.

STUDENT: If you let it go, it flies through the air.

MS. LANE: But what does that air do to the balloon?

STUDENT: Compresses it.

MS. LANE: Well, it makes that small balloon a lot bigger, right? So that air is compressed and you hear that word "pressed" in there . . . What happens if you don't tie that balloon and you let it go?

Here, Ms. Lane pauses to introduce the idea of air being compressed in a balloon, providing an opportunity for students to think about this idea in a new context.

ANCHORING LATER UNIT EXPERIENCES

Once introduced, "From Water Squirter to Super Soaker" serves as an anchor that supports teaching and learning throughout the remainder of the unit. After reading, Ms. Lane and her students use the text to inform how they design, test, and revise their toys in the classroom. In some instances, connections made to the text are seeded within the written curriculum (e.g., "Remind students about when they read about how Dr. Johnson designed the Super Soaker"); on other occasions, Ms. Lane's third-graders spontaneously draw these connections.

For example, while reading and discussing another text later in the unit, the "Balloon Rocket Text," one student notes that the characters' experiences building a toy balloon rocket remind her of the Super Soaker. Later in the unit, Ms. Lane supports students to recall what they read about Dr. Johnson to set the stage for supporting students to plan and conduct tests of their own toy designs and to support students to prepare design portfolios to share how they addressed the feedback from the kindergartners they interviewed earlier in the unit and used it to improve their final toy designs.

To illustrate this, when setting the stage for supporting students to plan and conduct tests of their own toy designs, Ms. Lane supports them to connect to Dr. Lonnie Johnson's experiences in the text by reminding students that "Lonnie Johnson . . . thought of some changes he wanted to make to his toy and then he had to go back and test it . . . you've thought about the changes you want to make to your toy to make it go faster, to make it more fun. So, what are we going to do now?" Students respond that now they need to test and improve their toys. Ms. Lane confirms, "Well, you're gonna make the change, and then what are you going to have to do? . . . Test it again."

This example illustrates how Ms. Lane and her students connect back to the ideas in this text in support of students learning and using engineering practices. While this type of coherence is seeded within the curriculum's design, it was achieved through Ms. Lane's instruction. Teachers create coherence by linking materials, experiences, and contexts in ways that enable students to make rich connections, particularly in the context of integrated instruction.[5] This illustrates how texts not only have the potential to provide opportunities for students to build knowledge about science and engineering practices, but also how ideas in the text might be productively leveraged throughout a project-based learning (PBL) unit in the service of new learning. Within Ms. Lane's class, this text (and others) provided the chance for the class to build shared knowledge and experiences, which Ms. Lane and her students were able to continue drawing on as they engaged in new experiences and learning throughout the unit.

MS. LANE'S REFLECTIONS ON TEACHING WITH TEXT

In an interview during her second year teaching the unit, Ms. Lane reflected on how she felt the class discussion went during the interactive read-aloud: "I thought it went great, like, too great . . . You had to kind of rein them back in." This illustrates the level of student engagement she observed while teaching with and discussing the text. She also reflected more holistically on the integration of literacy in ML-PBL, describing the ways in which the texts were integrally connected to students' firsthand experiences in the classroom:

> I—being more comfortable with [ML-PBL] this year—was able to just kind of see the excitement from them, whether it was a book, whether it was when they read something online. I mean, even some of their independent projects, they spun off of what we were doing in science . . . I walked into a first-grade classroom the week before the last week of school, and [the teacher] was standing at the front of the room with first graders—and they all had textbooks open—and . . . [lectured]. And I just thought of my own kids, and I thought, "The week before the last week of school?!" . . . I am so grateful that we don't have a textbook, that . . . we've got a variety of read-alouds that really connect with what we're doing.

Ms. Lane also speaks to evidence of her students' engagement across and beyond ML-PBL units by sharing how her students sought out additional texts related to what they were learning in the classroom. She shared: "Every time we went to the library, the kids would flock [to] the informational or the animals, or the birds, or cars and motion [foci related to the ML-PBL units]."

DISCUSSION

The design and Ms. Lane's enactment of the text "From Water Squirter to Super Soaker" provide insights into the selection and design of text in project-based science curricula, the integration of text and experience, and the role of the teacher in enacting curriculum materials to facilitate student learning.

Selection and Design of Text

This case illustrates the value of selecting and designing texts to draw on and extend students' uses of disciplinary core ideas, science and engineering practices, and crosscutting concepts to understand phenomena. In interviews, Ms. Lane spoke to the ways in which the design of "From Water Squirter to Super Soaker" and other ML-PBL texts drove student learning by supporting them to make connections to the Driving Question and other unit experiences and by providing information to support students in "tying things together" and "think[ing] about what they've learned."

Integration of Text and Experience

Instead of positioning the integrated literacy materials and activities as ends unto themselves, this case illustrates ways in which literacy tools were put to use in Ms. Lane's classroom in the service of connecting to, building on, and extending students' firsthand experiences to support students to build and apply usable science knowledge. Recall that, before reading, Ms. Lane engaged students in observing and investigating a variety of water squirters and the Super Soaker. During and after reading, Ms. Lane supported students to make connections to their own toy designs, uses of engineering practices, and experiences gathering feedback about their designs from kindergartners to improve their toys. This approach to integrating text and experience—engaging students in meaningful reading and literacy experiences during science instruction—has demonstrated promise for leading to greater comprehension gains than traditional school-based literacy activities, such as reading and writing without using information in meaningful ways.[6]

Role of the Teacher

Finally, we cannot ignore the integral role of the teacher in bringing designed opportunities for students to use multiple literacies in ML-PBL to life in the classroom. While the learning opportunities were instantiated within the curriculum materials, it was Ms. Lane's teaching with this text and other literacy resources that made opportunities for her students to use multiple literacies in the service of disciplinary knowledge building and science and engineering practice a reality. Ms. Lane made thoughtful choices about her teaching, such as choosing to extend students' firsthand observations and investigating the Super Soaker before reading the text and choosing to devote precious instructional time to ML-PBL across the school year. She felt this was important for realizing opportunities for her students to "engage in all aspects of the multiple literacies" and to allow "students with varying abilities to engage, explain, learn from, and demonstrate their learning and understanding of concepts."

CHAPTER 5

Integration of Technology in ML-PBL

KATHLEEN MARIE EASLEY, MIRANDA S. FITZGERALD, AND ANNEMARIE SULLIVAN PALINCSAR

It is a cold gray day in Michigan; nevertheless, there is a happy hum in Ms. Lawson's third-grade classroom. Her thirty-one students are immersed in the Toys Unit, in which they pursue the Driving Question, *How can we design fun moving toys that any kid can build?* They have made close observations of toy rockets launching, thinking about the forces at play. They have modeled their thinking and revised their models. Some of the children are designing their own rockets that will be propelled by forced air, while others are designing carts that will be pushed or pulled by an external force.

Throughout this unit, the students have been using digital technologies designed to support their efforts.[1] Importantly, these technologies level the playing field so all students have access to ideas that will be productive for their thinking.[2] Their work does not depend on their reading levels, and all students are supported in expressing their ideas, regardless of their writing skills.

INTRODUCING THE EDUCATIONAL CONTEXT

Ms. Lawson's third-grade classroom is brimming with color and life. A bulletin board at the back of the room reads "We Are Scientists." Students' scientific work is posted on the walls of the classroom and in the school hallways. Partially completed science projects line the counter. As a teacher, Ms. Lawson is passionate about providing students with engaging and high-quality science and literacy instruction. She requested to join the ML-PBL project after seeing a grade-level colleague enact the curriculum during the previous school year. At the time of this case study, Ms. Lawson was in her tenth year of teaching and her second year teaching with the ML-PBL materials. Before teaching third grade, Ms. Lawson taught middle school science.

Ms. Lawson typically taught from the ML-PBL curriculum four days a week, forty-five minutes per day. She was supported in her enactment of the ML-PBL materials by members of the ML-PBL research team. During the unit described in this case study, all of Ms. Lawson's science lessons were videorecorded, and the first author was present in Ms. Lawson's classroom several days a week.

This case study explores how Ms. Lawson supported her students to engage with three ML-PBL technology tools: *Flipbook*, a modeling tool; *WeRead*, which provides online access to texts including print text, illustrations, and videos and includes affordances such as text-to-speech so that students can listen to text being read aloud; and interactive simulations. As shown in this case, ML-PBL uses technology to support student interest and access to scientific concepts, access to multimedia representations, artifact creation, and collaboration.

VIGNETTE 1: IMPLEMENTING *WEREAD* TO SUPPORT ENGAGEMENT AND DIFFERENTIATION

It is early in the second semester. Students' desks are arranged into clusters of five. Above each cluster hangs a colored photograph of a planet; these photographs double as classroom decoration and group names. Today's lesson's Driving Question is, How can I start my toy moving? *Students will explore this Driving Question by using* WeRead *to research how to build a moving toy and then by building the toy.*

Ms. Lawson begins science class by reminding students that, on the previous day, they used instructional videos on WeRead *to help them sketch representations of the toy they planned to build and write a list of necessary materials. Ms. Lawson tells students that today they will review the* WeRead *instructional videos and collaborate to build a fun moving toy:*

> *[Yesterday], you labeled the materials you would need, and we watched the instruction videos. You'll need to watch those again today. Your goal today, with your group members, is to positively—with a positive attitude and working together, building that team—create your fun moving toy based on the instructions out of* WeRead.

Before dismissing students to work with WeRead, *Ms. Lawson makes sure that students who had previously been absent were assigned to a group. When assigning students to groups, Ms. Lawson makes thoughtful choices based on students' reading levels, interest in science, and background knowledge in science. She "purposefully groups" students to ensure that each group has someone who is motivated to learn about science and someone who can help any struggling readers. She also considers personality compatibility.*

Once every student has a group, each group gathers around a laptop, opens WeRead, *and navigates through the instructional readings and videos. Students access the toy-design instructions by reading the text out loud to each other, using the read-aloud feature of* WeRead, *or watching the instructional video.*

Ms. Lawson encourages students to use the WeRead *instructions to become experts on how to build their toy: "No [getting] materials until you've watched* WeRead *at least one time, because you cannot come back [to the material table] and tell me you don't know what you need. This is student led. You are telling us [the adults] what to do today." All groups spend five to seven minutes exploring the* WeRead *toy instructions before gathering materials and beginning construction.*

WeRead provides access to high-quality multimedia texts about key science ideas. In this example, students can use information drawn from *WeRead* to support building prototypes of moving toys that will be used throughout the unit to further understanding of the relationship between force and motion. Access to multimodal, digital resources supports students to collaborate to create their initial prototypes, using multiple representational forms. These multimodal forms also provide opportunities for students to make choices about the representations that best support their own toy designs. Building these initial prototypes sets the stage for the rest of the project-based learning (PBL) unit, in which students have opportunities to revise the design of their prototypes to improve their moving toys in pursuit of the Driving Question, *How can we design fun moving toys that any kid can build?* Later in the unit, other *WeRead* texts help students engage in investigations and learn more about the engineering design process.

In an interview, Ms. Lawson reported on students' engagement levels when reading on their Chromebooks: "I think the interest level rises when they can use their Chromebooks." She explained that the images and videos embedded in *WeRead* captured student attention and helped them to understand core ideas more deeply: "The *WeRead* that have images and videos attached, I've found they really get into that." She also shared that *WeRead* helped all students access the text because its read-aloud function provided access to students who might not otherwise be able to decode the text: "You click it, and then the robot reads to you."

However, Ms. Lawson also noted that no educational technology can replace the teacher. Supporting student reading comprehension was a key role that the teacher needed to play by supporting student understanding of key concepts and vocabulary through whole-class discussions and individual support: "You as the educator have to make sure that they're also doing the reading portion . . . if they don't understand some of the vocabulary, then it's our responsibility to make sure that they get that." When asked if there were any aspects of *WeRead* that were difficult for students, Ms. Lawson reported that some students had trouble highlighting and clicking text to activate the read-aloud function. However, she also shared, "I don't know how else you would do it [use the read-aloud function]."

VIGNETTE 2: IMPLEMENTING *FLIPBOOK* TO SUPPORT MODELING PHENOMENA AND DIFFERENTIATING INSTRUCTION

The second vignette illustrates how Ms. Lawson used *Flipbook* to create animated models. With this application, students can create representations of scientific phenomena such as how external forces impact the motion of a car. Students can then animate these representations by copying the original representation into new frames and making subtle changes between each of them. This creates a frame-by-frame animation that can show movement and change over time.

Today, Ms. Lawson's students are using their pencils and paper models as plans for creating animated models using the Flipbook *technology. Ms. Lawson reminds her students of the goal of the day's activity, which is to move from their paper models to creating a digital model showing why their toy starts and stops moving. As students receive their laptops, they open* Flipbook *and begin constructing their animated models. After students finish making their models, Ms. Lawson provides opportunities for them to share them with each other for feedback. Figure 5.1 provides examples of student models created during this time. Later in the unit, students will use their new knowledge of friction to revise their toy designs to increase the speed of their toy (for example, by introducing a lubricant, such as oil, into their toy system).*

FIGURE 5.1 ***Flipbook*** **pages depicting a model of the motion of a car propelled by a rubber band**

(1)

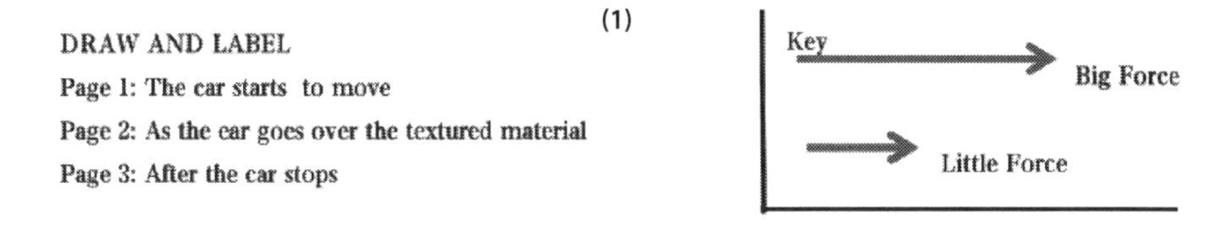

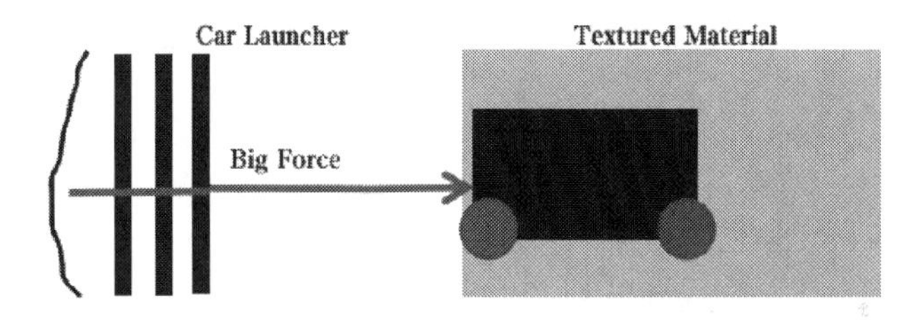

Type a few sentences to explain your model:

(2)

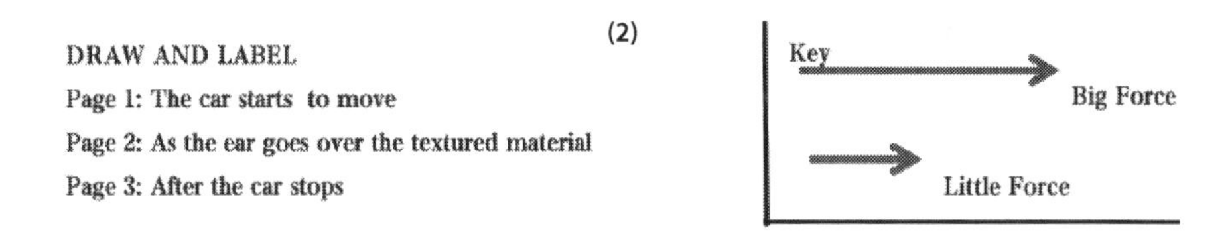

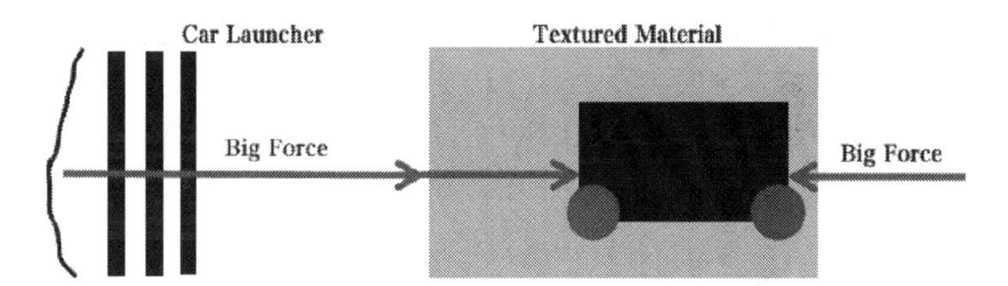

Type a few sentences to explain your model:

In frame (1), the student has shown the toy car being pushed by an initial starting force from a rubber band launcher. In frame (2), the rubber band is still applying a force and the textured material exerts an opposite force. The picture shows that the student understands that the initial starting force has caused the object to begin moving and that the frictional force from the textured material acts in an opposite direction to the initial force. However, the student also seems to believe that the rubber band continues to apply force even after it is no longer in contact with the car, which is not a scientifically accurate understanding. Because it can show both areas of understanding and areas of potential confusion, *Flipbook* allows the teacher to efficiently check the understanding of every student in the class. Thus, *Flipbook* supports the dual PBL goals of helping students construct artifacts that demonstrate their understanding of core concepts and supporting teachers to provide their students with targeted feedback and continued learning about core concepts.

Ms. Lawson also described a different technique that she has used with the *Flipbook* technology to assist students in working together with the aim of improving their models. She described it as a "mini science fair," where half the class stands by their computers while the other half walks around the room, taking on the role of the audience. The students switch roles between presenters and audience. As students circulate, they use sticky notes to leave each other suggestions and feedback. Ms. Lawson reported that giving feedback could be difficult for third-graders, who would often simply comment "It's great," without offering constructive suggestions for improvement. To support students to offer effective feedback, Ms. Lawson shared examples of what constructive suggestions might look like: for example, suggesting how part of their models can be expanded to show what effect the force is having on the toy. After the mini science fair, students return to their computers, read their peers' suggestions, and revise their models. Ms. Lawson explained that she prefers this "mini science fair" model of sharing and feedback because it provides more varied examples of student models, rather than sharing several student models where some students might modify their models like the examples.

Collaboration is a key aspect of PBL, and *Flipbook* offers unique affordances for collaboration both during model design and revision. In Ms. Lawson's classroom, students were often especially willing to revise their *Flipbook* models based on peer input, as compared to their willingness to revise their paper-and-pencil models.[3] Students' high levels of willingness to revise *Flipbook* models can be seen in Ms. Lawson's concern that, if all her students saw the same peer example, they might all choose to revise their model in the exact same way. Students' eagerness to collaboratively revise while using *Flipbook*, Ms. Lawson explains, is likely related to the way that *Flipbook* makes revisions both clean and easy, compared to the laborious and imperfect erasing and redrawing of a paper-and-pencil model. Also, the "undo" and "redo" features, which were used often by the students, allowed for quick revisions if they decided to change their designs.

When reflecting on the value of *Flipbook*, Ms. Lawson commented that it supported student engagement, especially for students who were particularly drawn toward visual representations: "I think for those kids that are visual or those kids that learn best using things like models, there's that high-interest piece behind Google Chromebooks and using Chromebooks."

Ms. Lawson reported that students who struggled in other areas were often successful when working with *Flipbook*. In particular, she reported that some of these students were able to take on a teaching role with this tool, supporting their classmates to use it more effectively. Ms. Lawson felt that *Flipbook* played an important role in helping all students to see themselves as successful scientists. She saw technology, with the affordances it provided for differentiation, as a key way of bringing all students into the science curriculum:

> I've noticed that some of my students that might be struggling in other areas really are able to shine when creating *Flipbooks*, or just that technology piece in general. I've had a few of my struggling readers whose brains worked in different ways, who were able to communicate their ideas through *Flipbook* or even teach other kids things that they had picked up . . . And so I think that's really important that each kid kind of sees themselves within our science studies. We want them understanding content. But at third grade, we also want them connecting with themselves as a science student.

Ms. Lawson shared that once *Flipbook* was introduced as part of ML-PBL, it spread to other parts of the school day. For example, students chose to use it when presenting at the school STEM fair. One student's STEM fair entry included a volcano, a poster explaining the volcano, and a *Flipbook* that used images and labels to show the mixture that created the volcanic reaction. She also reported that other educators who visited the science fair asked how they could use *Flipbook* in their classrooms: "Anybody that visits is always like, 'Wow! How do we get this going in our room?'"

She also shared that students enjoyed using *Flipbook* when creating their own research projects during independent work time:

> I think *Flipbook* definitely lends [itself] to . . . allowing that creative piece. I mean, think about it. So, let's say they decided to study chameleons or something. And usually with an independent project, outside of the curriculum, they

> are going to create a flowchart of some kind or an interaction model on paper. Instead, they can do that in *Flipbook*, right? And so, you get that deeper level, because they're going to go deeper with that [*Flipbook*] than just writing things down on paper . . . that's going to be high interest for them.

When asked if there were any challenges related to *Flipbook*, Ms. Lawson shared two observations. First, students sometimes struggled with technical aspects of the program. For example, they sometimes found it difficult to select and rotate an entire object and would become frustrated when they were only able to select a small subset of the object. Second, she found that students could be distracted by the feature that allowed them to import photographs. While she did feel there were advantages in students developing internet search skills, she also felt that importing photographs from the internet could be distracting and detract from the authenticity of students' models.

VIGNETTE 3: IMPLEMENTING THE "NET FORCE SIMULATION" IN SUPPORT OF NGSS PRACTICES AND DIFFERENTIATION

The third vignette illustrates how Ms. Lawson used an interactive online simulation to explore concepts related to net force. The Net Force Simulation is an open-access simulation designed by PhET.[4] It depicts a game of tug-of-war in which students manipulate the number and size of people on each side of a rope. As they change the number and size of the pullers, the brown arrows representing left and right force shift accordingly. After predicting the motion of the cart, students can press "Go" to find out which direction, if any, the cart will move once the pullers start tugging.

It is midafternoon, and Ms. Lawson is teaching a ML-PBL lesson that supports students to understand the connection between unbalanced forces and movement. The day's Driving Question is: How can I use a model to predict how different forces can change the motion of the toy? *Ms. Lawson's class has been working with the Net Force Simulation for about half an hour. Most of the students are sitting cross-legged on the floor in front of the interactive whiteboard. Behind these students, a few more students sit on chairs, also facing the interactive whiteboard.*

The interactive whiteboard is currently showing the starting screen of the Net Force Simulation. The cart sits in the middle of the screen, with a rope extending from each side. Ms. Lawson invites Sari to come up to the board and place one figure on each side of the rope, suggesting that Sari choose figures of different sizes. Sari chooses a medium figure from the left side and a small figure from the right side. Ms. Lawson invites her students to consider whether the forces are balanced or unbalanced and whether the cart will move or not. One student shares a prediction that the cart will move because one side has bigger people. Most students give a thumbs up as an indication that they agree with this prediction. Ms. Lawson then invites Sari to hit "Go." The class observes as the cart moves in the direction of the medium figure and away from the smaller figure, as predicted. Ms. Lawson then invites the class to explain why the cart moved.

"Here's my question for you. What kind of force was created when Sari put a larger stick guy against the smaller? What kind of force to make that cart move?" Students share that the cart is moving because the forces were unbalanced, with more force on one side of the cart.

Later, the class explores a scenario with balanced forces. Jonathan stands in front of the interactive whiteboard, trying to place people of various sizes onto each side of the rope. However, nothing happens. Ms. Lawson steps up beside Jonathan to help. She stands away from the interactive whiteboard, careful not to block her students' view of the screen. She demonstrates how to use a "hold-down, slide, and release" motion to move the people onto the rope. "You have to push and slide," she tells Jonathan. Jonathan tries to move the people again, successfully moving the figures onto the rope. Ms. Lawson nods: "There you go!"

Jonathan places a large figure, a medium figure, and two small figures on one side of the cart. He places a large figure, a medium figure, and two small figures on the other side of the cart. Ms. Lawson turns to the class to ask about the amount of force (measured in newtons) that is pulling on the right side of the cart: "Okay, now, notice what is the value heading toward the right. What's the newtons?[5] *What's that assigned value?"*

Multiple students raise their hands. Ms. Lawson calls on George.

George looks up at the simulation screen and reads the number printed on the arrow pointing left: "Three hundred and fifty," he replies.

"Three hundred and fifty newtons pulling toward the right," agrees Ms. Lawson. "Jonathan? What do you have over there for left?"

From his position next to the interactive whiteboard, Jonathan leans in to look at the number printed on the arrow pointing left. "The same thing," he says.

Ms. Lawson addresses the whole class. "What do we think right now?" she asks. "Put a thumb up if you think it's going to be balanced and not go anywhere."

The class has already tested multiple simulation scenarios with equal force pulling in each direction. In every such case, students have observed that the forces have been balanced and the cart has not moved. In response to Ms. Lawson's question, most students put their thumbs up, predicting that the force is balanced and the cart will not move. However, some students seem unsure and do not put their thumbs up. Ms. Lawson tells Jonathan to "Go ahead and hit 'Go.'"

Jonathan hits "Go." All the figures lean backward as they begin to try to move the cart. The cart doesn't budge. The class erupts into giggles. Ms. Lawson poses a question to the entire class. "Why doesn't it go anywhere?" There is silence. "They're all pulling," Ms. Lawson continues. "The force is there! But that cart is not going anywhere."

Sara raises her hand. "'Cause it's a balanced . . . "

"Because it's a balanced force," Ms. Lawson says, expanding on Sara's response. "How do I know that it's a balanced force?"

Mary raises her hand.

Ms. Lawson calls on Mary, who looks at the simulation screen carefully, but doesn't share an answer.

"What do you see up here?" Ms. Lawson prompts.

"They're all the same," says Mary.

"They're all the same size," Ms. Lawson agrees. "And we decided that, for this simulation, size did mean how much force."

Ms. Lawson then goes on to tell her students that they are almost out of time for science. However, she also lets them know that they will be continuing their work with the simulation on the following Monday. Furthermore, she shares that on Monday, students will each have their own laptop and will be able to experiment with the simulation independently. While the students seem disappointed to be wrapping up their whole-class simulation investigation, they also seem excited about their upcoming independent exploration.

In this third vignette, we see Ms. Lawson using the simulation to support Next Generation Science Standards (NGSS) scientific practices, including using simulations, interpreting data, making claims supported by reasoning, and communicating information. Students use the interactive simulation to set up and test scenarios, interpreting the features of the simulation, including the size of the pullers and the numbers on the arrows. They describe the results of their scenario (no movement of the cart), explain why this result occurred (balanced forces on each side of the cart), and share information about the simulation with each other, supported by Ms. Lawson's prompts. We also see Ms. Lawson differentiating instruction. For example, she adjusts her prompts when Mary seems confused in order to help Mary share her ideas with the class.

This vignette shows multiple affordances of the simulation. First, Ms. Lawson uses the simulation to support students to figure out the relationship between unbalanced forces and movement, a core idea in the Toys Unit. Students later apply this increased understanding of force and motion toward designing and testing their final toy; many students leveraged their knowledge of unbalanced forces to create a toy that moved farther and/or faster. For example, several students decided they wanted to power their water-bottle rocket with a larger bottle to increase the magnitude of the starting force. Second, the simulation lesson supports sustained investigation across lessons and over time, another fundamental tenet of PBL.[6] The simulation-based lesson is synergistic with other hands-on investigations that explore the same topic.[7]

Third, Ms. Lawson uses the simulation to give students an opportunity to interpret data from a multimodal visual representation, which is valued within the context of PBL.[8] In particular, we see this when she invites students to consider the relationship between the features of the simulation (e.g., the numbers and arrows) and the conceptual ideas that the simulation represents (e.g., force). Both the NGSS and the National Research Council's *Framework for K–12 Science Education* specifically recommend supporting students to interpret models, including simulations.[9] Finally, there is the ease and accuracy with which the simulation can be used, compared to enacting an actual tug-of-war between the students.

When asked if there were any challenges associated with using the simulations, Ms. Lawson identified that the main difficulty arose from issues with hardware: the interactive whiteboard was not always reliable. Ms. Lawson also mentioned certain simplifications that had the potential to confuse students. For example, in the Net Force Simulation, the strength of the figures pulling on the rope is always proportionate to their size, whereas in real life, someone's size and strength are not necessarily proportionate. However, Ms. Lawson did not necessarily consider this to be a problem in the simulation. Instead, she felt that it offered the opportunity for students to discuss the limits of representations.

AFFORDANCES OF TECHNOLOGY FOR SUPPORTING PBL

Each of the technology tools in this case study had a part to play in supporting key features of ML-PBL or PBL, including sustained sensemaking over time, creation of a final artifact, and sustained inquiry over time in pursuit of a Driving Question. This case study has particularly considered how technology supported sensemaking in the context of the Toys Unit, which focused on concepts related to force and motion. Each of the technologies used in the vignettes above supported students to understand force and motion. The readings, videos, and images that students accessed through *WeRead* provided the foundations for many discussions that were rich in sensemaking. *Flipbook* provided students the opportunity to design animated models showing the relationship between force and motion. The simulations provided students with the opportunity to engage in simulated investigations of the relationship between force and motion. These technology-supported inquiry opportunities synergized with hands-on inquiry throughout the unit, giving students robust opportunities to both investigate the relationship between force and motion and use their learning to build and improve fun moving toys.

Building Toward a Final Artifact

At the end of the Toys Unit, students redesigned their toy to improve its movement and tested whether or not their new design outperformed their original model. Each of the technology-based opportunities described above played a role in supporting the design, testing, and redesign of students' toys. *WeRead* supported students during the initial building process. The simulations supported students to identify the relationship between force and movement, which in turn prompted ideas for how to increase the toy's movement by increasing the starting force. *Flipbook* prompted ideas for how to increase a toy's movement by decreasing friction. Together, the technology-based opportunities in the ML-PBL unit played a pivotal role in supporting students' creation of the final artifact.

Collaboration Among Students

The digital technology tools incorporated into the ML-PBL curriculum supported student collaboration, each in its own way. Students used the multiple modalities of information available in *WeRead* as a resource while collaboratively constructing their toy models. The online simulation provided fodder for collaborative discussions and co-construction of claims. *Flipbook* provided the opportunity for students to revise their models, drawing on suggestions from their peers. Taken together, the technology tools incorporated into the ML-PBL curriculum supported students to collaboratively engage in hands-on investigation (e.g., by supporting the construction of the initial toys), to collaboratively engage in claim construction (e.g., by discussing simulation results), and to collaboratively engage in model revision (i.e., using *Flipbook*). These technology-supported collaboration opportunities complement other opportunities for collaboration woven throughout the ML-PBL units.

TECHNOLOGIES AND THE TEACHER'S ROLE

Ms. Lawson spoke of technology as enhancing, rather than replacing, teaching. When students worked at their computers, she never remained seated. Instead, she circulated among the students, troubleshooting technical issues, supporting conceptual understanding, and helping students remain focused on conceptual parts of their work. Examples of troubleshooting technical issues included assisting students who were having trouble connecting to the internet, using the read-aloud function on *WeRead*, and rotating objects using *Flipbook*. Examples of supporting students' conceptual understanding included having whole-class discussions about concepts from the *WeRead* readings or simulations. An example of supporting student focus was monitoring how much time students spent searching for images when using *Flipbook*. Overall, Ms. Lawson saw her role as supporting students' understanding; while technology could assist, it could never take the teacher's place.[10]

LIMITATIONS OF THE TECHNOLOGY

For each of the tools discussed in this case study, Ms. Lawson identified potential limitations. In some cases, these limitations were related to features of the tool that students had difficulty operating. For example, students sometimes had difficulty selecting objects in *Flipbook* or highlighting text in *WeRead*. In other cases, the limitations were conceptual. Ms. Lawson identified simplifications in the simulation's underlying model that had the potential to lead to confusion if not addressed. A further set of limitations was related to the infrastructure in Ms. Lawson's classroom, such as problems with the interactive whiteboard or internet connection.

FINAL THOUGHTS ON THE USE OF ML-PBL TECHNOLOGY IN ONLINE LEARNING

Prompted by necessary changes in schooling due to the COVID-19 pandemic, many elementary teachers moved to online or hybrid models of instruction. For this reason, we conclude this chapter by reflecting on the potential for the ML-PBL digital technology's use in online or hybrid instruction. Each of the tools mentioned in this chapter (*Flipbook*, *WeRead*, and the PhET simulations) is available online for free. Furthermore, these tools are device agnostic, meaning that they can be used on laptops, Chromebooks, tablets, and many other devices. In classes using ML-PBL, all teachers and students could have individual and free access to all technology described in this chapter, provided all students have access to both technology (Chromebook, laptop, and other devices) and the internet. Students could support toy building at home using recycled materials, conduct investigations using online simulations, and design and share models using *Flipbook*. *Flipbook* has an additional feature, not used in Ms. Lawson's classroom, in which two or more students can work together on the same model while using different computers. This feature could be particularly helpful to support collaboration in online learning situations. Students could either use the ML-PBL tools asynchronously, following guidance provided by the teacher, or they could interact with ML-PBL technology tools while simultaneously conversing with classmates and teacher via video conferencing.

While the use of ML-PBL technology to support remote learning has not yet been empirically tested, its in-classroom use suggests that it offers strong potential to support remote PBL that adheres to fundamental tenants of PBL, including: meaningful sensemaking, sustained inquiry in support of a Driving Question, collaboration, and production of a final artifact based on student learning throughout the unit.

CHAPTER 6

Developing Deep Learning Through Systems Thinking

TINGTING LI

Ms. Kramer, an elementary school science teacher with fifteen years' experience, is exploring with her class how squirrels survive outside without being taken care of by humans. The class has already looked for squirrels in the neighborhood by the school. They used binoculars and observation data sheets to keep track of what they observed squirrels doing. Ms. Kramer has a piece of chart paper with the title "Squirrel Needs" underlined. She asks the students the Driving Question for this lesson: What can we observe about squirrels and how they survive outside? She reviews the word observation with the students and directs their attention to their fieldnotes. "Jacob said that squirrels need to eat food to survive. Look at your notes. Did anyone see the squirrel eating food?" Alison pipes up: "I saw it running around the tree. I think it was looking for food." Another student disagrees. He suggests that the squirrel was playing. Alex, studying his notes, wonders how squirrels get enough to eat. "Where does he get his food? I mean, where does it come from?" Ms. Kramer asks him to say more. Alex continues, wondering out loud, "When people don't feed seeds to the squirrel, it will die." He pauses, "Will it die?" Ms. Kramer asks Alex to write his question down on a large index card. She will add this question to the Driving Question Board for the class to grapple with together. She knows that the students will gradually figure out that animals survive outside because the environment works as a system.

This episode is from the beginning of the Squirrels Unit and foreshadows the complex thinking the students will be using as they learn to use ideas to explain the relationships between the survival of organisms, their diversity, and ecosystems: big ideas related to systems thinking, which is foundational in the field of ecology. When students apply systems thinking to make sense of phenomena and solve complex problems, they must identify the relationships between various interconnected components that make up a system and describe how the system works.[1] The construction of scientific models to explain phenomena provides additional opportunities for students to show their thinking about these components; moreover, they can use the models to figure out and test the relationships among the components. However, using systems thinking and constructing models is challenging, especially for elementary students with limited experiences using scientific practices like investigations and developing models. Yet the development of systems and system modeling—a crosscutting concept in the NGSS—*can* happen, as shown in Ms. Kramer's classroom, where she supports her students in applying systems thinking and constructing system models to explain complex problems and phenomena. She begins this process in the Squirrels Unit and follows it through the third-grade Multiple Literacies in Project-Based Learning (ML-PBL) units, deepening the students' use of these ideas.

MAKING SENSE OF SQUIRRELS' SURVIVAL USING SYSTEMS THINKING

At the beginning of the Squirrels Unit, students observe squirrels and use their observations to construct a list of squirrels' survival needs. They connect those needs to the observations they collected outside. Ms. Kramer instructs her students to work together in small groups and use the list to draw a picture that shows how the squirrels meet one of their needs. She then leads a discussion in which students offer ideas based on their small-group work. Together, the class constructs an initial group consensus model that shows how the environment provides all that the squirrel needs for survival, including water, food, protection, and warmth. This initial experience builds the foundation for students to engage in systems thinking and system modeling.[2]

Near the end of this first ML-PBL science unit, Ms. Kramer supports her students in synthesizing ideas to develop models that explain the extinction of the stegosaurus. This model must use the idea of systems working together, as in the squirrel model; here, however, the goal is to show how, if a need is not met, the organism will not survive. Ms. Kramer gathers her students into small groups and asks them to take out the models they started in the previous class.

She reads the lesson's Driving Question: *Can we use our model to explain our thinking about what happened to the stegosaurus?*

As students continue their work on their models, Ms. Kramer speaks with each student individually. With their small groups, the students will present a play or a story about how the extinction event might have occurred, and they must draw on their individual models to put together this final artifact. Ms. Kramer poses questions to her class to help them think deeply about what components and relationships are needed to explain why the stegosaurus became extinct: "What specific events may have caused the stegosaurus to become extinct?"; "What made the stegosaurus disappear before all of the other dinosaurs?"; "What changes in the environment may have caused them to disappear?"; and "What about weather conditions that could have had an effect? Predators? Safety of animals in a group versus individuals?" These questions support students in identifying the components necessary for their models. To further support her students' learning, Ms. Kramer writes on the whiteboard: "Organism Systems > Everything works together." By writing this statement, she signals to the students that their models need to show how all parts are connected to each other in the system.

Here, Ms. Kramer is supporting students in using the lens of systems thinking to explain the extinction of the stegosaurus, asking questions about components that may affect their survival, and providing consistent feedback using a system model by emphasizing relationships between those components. Ms. Kramer is cognizant that the crosscutting concept of systems and systems thinking is invaluable for supporting her students with this challenging idea in ecology. Upon completion of the Squirrels Unit, when asked which key aspects of project-based learning (PBL) she thinks supports students' science learning, Ms. Kramer responds,

> Discussion really helps them understand how things work together because I think sometimes we take for granted the reasons why something is that way. And you just kind of—just, "Well, because it always is!" And ML-PBL has them slow down and think about it, and understand more completely about the things around them and how they interact and what we can do to help change things or to add to things.

Here, Ms. Kramer's use of the word *interact* refers to how organisms in a system affect other organisms in the environment. She explains how she uses discussion to foster students' understanding of these interactions and relationships, and how the addition or subtraction of different components can change a system.

APPLYING SYSTEMS THINKING IN THE SQUIRRELS UNIT ASSESSMENT

At the end of every unit, there is a unit formative assessment that is designed to be aligned with the performance expectations in the NGSS. For example, in the Squirrels Unit, the students are tasked with imagining the effect on squirrels if trees are removed from the ecosystem. Additionally, these assessments are formative and require students to show how well they have mastered the disciplinary core ideas, such as organisms' relationships to one another's survival, and biodiversity; the scientific practices of constructing models, data analysis, and conducting an investigation; and crosscutting concepts, systems and system models, and cause and effect.[3] Specifically, the Squirrels Unit post-assessment targets students' ability to use all three dimensions to develop a model of how a squirrel might or might not survive if its ecosystem is missing a key component.

The Squirrels Unit post-assessment consists of five tasks. In the first task, the students are shown a picture of a squirrel in a forest. They are then asked to draw a model of what could happen to the Eastern Gray Squirrels that live in this forest if all of the trees are cut down. The context of this task presents a new situation that students did not experience in the unit. To offer a more complete picture of their understanding, students also provide a written explanation of their model. The representation of the students' thinking (the model) combined with their written explanation offers a window into their thinking, to support the teacher in accurately assessing what ideas each student has mastered.

To receive the highest grade, a student's response must include components in the system that could affect the squirrels' survival, show the relationships among components, and depict what happened to the squirrels' survival based on these relationships.[4]

Figure 6.1 presents a response typical of many of Ms. Kramer's students. The model and explanation include components of the system that could affect the squirrels' survival, such as "tree," "food," "habitat," and "predators." The drawing shows relationships between these components that may affect the squirrels' survival: "If there is no tree, the squirrel has no food; they will have no place to

FIGURE 6.1 A student's predictive model about the squirrels' survival

Explain your model.

Here is one idea that might be helpful in writing your answer.

- ***If the habitat changes, it will impact the animals that live there.***

If there is no trees there will be no oxygan

no place to hide.

hide; and they will have no place to live in." This student's response does not include how these relationships correspond to whether or not the squirrels survive. Nevertheless, although it misses an important relationship, it does show how the student reacted to a new scenario and attempted to explain how changes in the environment affect an organism's survival using system modeling.

FIGURING OUT THE RELATIONSHIP BETWEEN FORCE AND MOTION USING SYSTEMS THINKING

Ms. Kramer further uses systems and systems thinking as a lens through which students can understand the phenomenon of why a toy car stops, moves, or changes direction in the next unit, Toys Unit. This is an added challenge because, unlike squirrels, some of the components in the system are abstract and unseen: balanced and unbalanced forces.

It is the beginning of November, and the students have completed eight weeks of the Squirrels Unit. Ms. Kramer is in the middle of a lesson on how toys move when forces are unbalanced—another challenging idea for elementary learners. The students have already investigated the movement of a toy that they pushed with their hand, and now they are considering unseen pushes and pulls and the relative directions and strengths of those forces on the same toy. Ms. Kramer begins the lesson by articulating the lesson's Driving Question, "Today, we are going to explain how our toy cars can move without us touching them. Okay. So, remember, we're going to be drawing a model of this. So make sure you understand every part of the system here, and everything that we're doing and how everything's interacting. Okay?"

Ms. Kramer has created a bridge with a stiff sheet of cardboard that is held up by two blocks, one on either side. She places the car on the cardboard bridge. "Now, when I place the car in the center of the bridge made with the stiff cardboard, does the car move?" The class responds "No," with some students shaking their heads. Then she poses the question, "Think to yourself: Is this a balance or an unbalanced force acting on the car?" Alex shouts out, "It is balanced—the car is not moving." Smiling, Ms. Kramer says, "Okay, so now I am going to exchange the single flat sheet with a flexible sheet of cardboard and put the car on the bridge. What happened?" Shira answers, "The car moved." Ms. Kramer continues: "Now, class, turn to your partner and ask each other why that happened."

After listening to the students talking with their partners, Ms. Kramer says, "I am hearing some good conversation. Well, what did we come up with?" Jason exclaims, "The car started to move down when placed on the flexible sheet of cardboard, because it is thinner and the car is heavier." Ms. Kramer asks the class if everyone agrees. Some of the students nod their heads in agreement, but some disagree. Building on earlier lessons that involved modeling, Ms. Kramer asks, "If we wanted to draw a model of the car moving down, what might we do?" Maddy responds, "We should have a longer arrow pointing down when the car moved and a shorter arrow pointing up because the force up is not as strong as the force pulling the car down." "Well, that is interesting," Ms. Kramer replies. "Do we agree with Maddy? With your group, see what a model of the car might look like if it is in an unbalanced state." The students take out their notebooks, conferring with one another as they begin drawing their models.

In the above description, we see how Ms. Kramer's third-grade students become more adept at using systems thinking to show parts of a system that work together to cause a car not to move and comparing that system to one with a changed component that caused motion to occur. With the lesson's Driving Question in mind, Ms. Kramer reminds her students of the investigation they completed previously and the models they built about that phenomenon. She asks them to discuss with a partner the importance of knowing what forces are acting on their toys; moreover, she instructs them to discuss how these models work by using the relationships between components to explain this new phenomenon.

In this sequence, similar to the modeling activity in the Squirrels Unit, Ms. Kramer emphasizes systems and system models to support her students' learning. Before placing a toy car on the rigid bridge, she reminds her students to make sure they understand every part of the system and asks them to identify the relevant components within the system. To support them, she focuses on visible objects in the system and then brings in the components that are unseen. Ms. Kramer supports the students in modeling these components in the system through questioning. She needs to make the connections explicit for the students because of the added complexity of this model compared to the squirrel model, the extinction model, and the first model of a car moving when pushed by a hand.

As she places the toy car on the rigid bridge, she asks, "Is this a balanced or an unbalanced force?" Ela responds, "I think it is balanced." Ms. Kramer replies, "How do you know?" He answers, "Because nothing is moving." Ms. Kramer uses this opportunity to have her students represent the relationships among the parts in the system: "Okay, so there's nothing moving. There's no motion—I want you to think about it. Remember when we did the tug-of-war simulation.[5] Think about those arrows. Remember what the arrows showed? And, like, what did they do to the arrows when everything was equal? Malisa?" Malisa responds,

"They made the arrows the same size." Ms. Kramer restates Malisa's comment: "So, you had arrows on each side, and they were both the same size and shape." She then discusses with the class how to represent forces with different directions and strengths using different-sized arrows and paying attention to arrow direction. They agree that longer arrows should represent bigger forces and shorter arrows represent smaller forces, and that arrows should point in the direction of those forces.

Ms. Kramer directs the students to think about the lesson's Driving Questions: "[Today's] Driving Questions were, *How can we make our toy move down without touching it?* right? And, *How can we explain how it can move down without touching it?* All right, so what would the arrows look like on this model?" Manny replies by using her hands to illustrate the direction of the forces: "Maybe there will be like small arrows from the bottom, and then some longer arrows going down from the top." Ms. Kramer turns to other students and asks them to repeat, add, or clarify Manny's idea. After several students have responded, Ms. Kramer asks, "What direction would you put the arrows underneath? Is the direction of the motion going [down] towards the table? Or is it going up toward the car?" Several students raise their hand, responding "Up toward the car." Some students quickly refute, "Down!"

Ms. Kramer supports her students in learning about systems and system models and in understanding the ideas related to forces and motion by observing the car's movement: linking it back to the Driving Question about how and why the car starts moving and showing the relationships between the forces acting on the bridge and the car using arrows with different directions and sizes. Here, she uses Gina's idea to explore how a model can be used to show the behavior of system. Gina, talking about forces acting on the car and how they would be shown in a model, says, "I think that both of the arrows would be going down. I think the reason that the longer arrows would be going down [is] because there's more motion, but the smaller arrows on the bottom would still be going down. Because the car would be pushing down." Ms. Kramer focuses the conversation on how the car moved down and what forces acted on it during the process. The students examine the relationship between the force pulling the car down and the force pushing it up, including both the strength and direction of the forces; moreover, they use their own words to express their understanding. In this manner, Ms. Kramer's students further develop their understanding of systems thinking as well as ideas of balanced and unbalanced forces.

In this example, systems thinking becomes an essential aspect of sophisticated three-dimensional learning. Throughout the process, visible components (such as the car, cardboard, and blocks) are discussed, but abstract scientific ideas (such as the forces acting on the car) are also emphasized. Yet without the use of a system model, neither of these dimensions can be applied to understanding the phenomenon of a car moving without a physical push. In this way, students' understanding of system components extends to everything in the system that affects the motion of the car. In addition, the supportive learning environment allows students to communicate with their peers and struggle together to extend their lens of systems and system models to a new scientific discipline.

APPLYING SYSTEMS THINKING IN THE TOYS UNIT ASSESSMENT

Responses from the Toys Unit show students using systems thinking and applying a sophisticated understanding of balanced and unbalanced forces to explain phenomena. In the Toys Unit assessment, students were asked to describe and draw all forces acting on the car when it is at rest. Figure 6.2 shows the response of one student, which is representative of the other students' responses. It shows the forces acting on the car, including contact force (with upward-pointing arrows between the car and the table), gravity all around the car, and the friction between the car and the table. The response illustrates how the student is explaining the phenomenon using the lens of systems thinking through examining the interactions between various forces in the system. Although the direction of gravity is not shown accurately, given the complexity and abstraction of the concept, the response is appropriate.

Another item in the assessment asks students to use a list of materials—magnets, balloons, paper clips, a hair dryer, and felt cloth—to change the car design so that when two cars are pushed into one another, they stop immediately. Students are asked to first provide their design plan, then draw their design and explain how it works. One student chose a magnet from the list to change the car design. The student wrote, "Put the magnet on the car, then put the other magnet by it, so it will stop." The model the student drew includes the components that can affect the car's motion. Although the solution does not describe

FIGURE 6.2 Model of forces acting on the car

2 The yellow car is at rest. Describe **all of the forces** that are acting on the car when it is at rest.

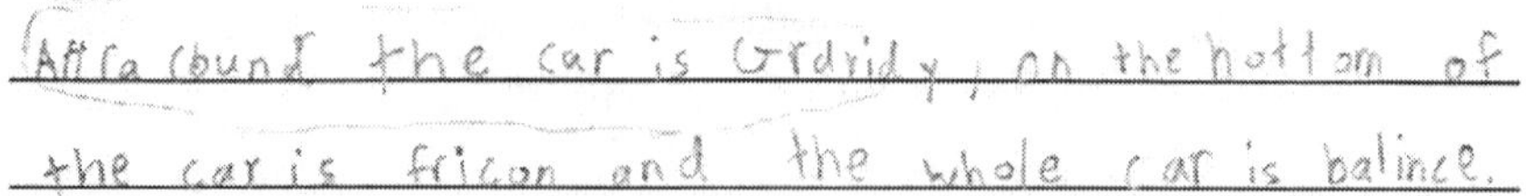

3 Now draw the yellow car and the forces acting on it when it is at rest. Make sure you show if the forces are **balanced** or **unbalanced.**

the relationships among those components, the written explanation indicates them and further explains how the design works: "It will stop because when you bring out a magnet by the other, it pulls it and then it will stop moving." The word "pull" implicitly presents a relationship between the force that was used to push the car and the force that two magnets applied to each other. By describing the relationship between the two forces, the student provides an explanation about why the design stops the car. This student is applying the ideas of balanced and unbalanced force to solve problems by identifying the components in the system that affect the car's motion and stating the relationships among those components.

BUILDING AND PLACEMENT OF A BIRD FEEDER USING SYSTEMS THINKING

The Birds Unit, the third ML-PBL unit., brings together all the ideas, practices, and crosscutting concepts from earlier units to consider the impact of an engineered solution on an ecosystem, as well as on individual components of that ecosystem. In this unit, the students engineer a solution to bring about a desired change to their local environment (the system). The planned solution is a student-created artifact for helping local birds that affects the system. The unit and the context of systems thinking challenge the students to extend their prior learning to describe a hypothetical scenario, with one component—a bird feeder—added only at the end of the unit.

Throughout the Birds Unit, students make decisions about the design and placement of a bird feeder by identifying components in the system that could affect the birds' ability to thrive and reproduce and successfully raise offspring. Components in this system include the birds' physical and behavioral traits, the changing weather, the birds' social behavior, the features of the environment, and the birds' needs for reproduction. The students examine the relationships between these components, identify a problem that they can help with, and describe how their solution response to the system. Students observe the birds' feeding and foraging behavior and do text-based "research" to figure out what, if any, changes in the placement of the feeder are needed to assure that it will attract birds. Small groups discuss where their bird feeder should be sited and create a timeline to understand the pattern of change in the birds' behavior during the day and throughout the year, including migration. Students thus synthesize their information not just to design a bird feeder but also to decide where it would be most effectively placed.

Ms. Kramer begins class by telling her students that they will design bird feeders for their focal birds and make decisions about where they should place them. She reads the lesson Driving Question aloud: *"Considering all we have learned, where should we place our bird feeders?"* She draws her students' attention to the Driving Question Board and reminds them to think about what they have already learned to make informed decisions about their bird feeders' design. Students had already explored websites to obtain information about whether their focal bird forages on the ground or perches on a branch; they have also discussed how to design a feeder. In this lesson, they consider where to place the feeder using the information they have gathered and their observations. As the third-graders work on their design, Ms. Kramer reminds them to consider their bird's physical and behavioral traits.

In subsequent classes, students engage in an iterative redesign process as they come up with new ideas based on what they learn. Ms. Kramer tells her students that they must make a decision about the type of food their focal bird will need (in addition to how their bird will access that food) and then complete the construction of the feeder. Again, Ms. Kramer asks her students to think about how their birds forage for food and what they eat. The class goes outside to observe and make decisions regarding whether to use wire or twine to hang the feeder to withstand weather conditions. Here, Ms. Kramer scaffolds her students to think about the bird feeder design—still hypothetical—and its relationship with the known components in the system. They have to figure out the placement of the bird feeder considering what they know about the complex system. She encourages students to consider the external factors, such as weather conditions and their focal bird's traits.

After completing the Birds Unit, when asked how she saw her students making connections between ML-PBL and their lives and communities, Ms. Kramer responds,

> I think they were starting to realize the connection between animal survival and interactions with other things, especially ourselves, because we were helping them survive with our feeders we were building. I think part of that was having them understand we are all connected, and we have to make things like safe environments for people and animals, and [have] the supplies to survive and things that you need, like the food and everything. I think they really made that connection.

Ms. Kramer expresses the progression that her students have followed to use systems thinking and an engineering solution. The engineering experience of toy car building, the idea of squirrels' survival, and the characteristics of birds have all been integrated to provide systems thinking regarding the bird feeder design and placement.

APPLYING SYSTEMS THINKING IN THE BIRDS UNIT ASSESSMENT

The first item on the Birds Unit post-assessment provides information through text and pictures about birds of two different species. The information includes the birds' physical traits and the food they eat. The length of brown-headed cowbird adult is 16–22 cm, while the cedar waxwing adult is 15–18 cm. Brown-headed cowbirds feed mostly in seeds and grains. Insects such as grasshoppers and beetles make up about a quarter of a cowbird's diet. Cedar waxwings feed on fruits such as strawberries, mulberries, and raspberries in summer. The bird gets its name from its appetite for cedar berries in winter; they also eat mistletoe, juniper, mountain ash, honeysuckle, and crabapple fruits.

Students are presented with a scenario in which a cedar waxwing mother has laid eggs in her nest, and a brown-headed cowbird has laid eggs in that same nest and then left. The task prompts students to think about what they know about birds' traits (their behavior and what they look like), and how birds live in their environments. Students need to make a prediction about what they think will happen when the cedar waxwing brings food to the chicks and then draw a model with an explanation to show their prediction, including evidence regarding what will help or hurt the two different birds' chances of survival. To provide an appropriate response to the question, simply memorizing the facts of the birds' physical traits or their eating habits is insufficient: here, students must apply their knowledge to a new situation, using the lens of systems thinking. Figure 6.3, below, shows a typical example of how students responded.

In figure 6.3, the prediction, model, and explanation show different components of the system, including the cedar waxwing mother, cedar waxwing chicks, cowbird chicks, and the food brought by the cedar waxwing mother. In this assessment, it is the relationship among the components (e.g., bird behavior) that must be brought forward and explored by the students to make the prediction of the system make sense. The students must use evidence to explain how the cowbird would (or would not) survive. The model and explanation shown in figure 6.3 present the two possible relationships between different components in the system. In the first, the cedar waxwing mother brings berries to the chicks, but the cowbird chicks will not eat the berries. The different species of chicks eat different food and have different physical characteristics and dietary needs. In the second, the student uses a scientific idea of behavior to show a relationship between survival and inherited behavioral characteristics. If the cowbird has survived through generations by placing eggs in other birds' nests, then there is reason to believe that this inherited behavior would be the result of the cowbird chicks' successful development. With this system, a student might show that the behavior allows a cowbird to deposit many eggs in many nests without expending energy to raise all of them.

FIGURE 6.3 Model predicting the birds' survival

2. **Draw a model** to show your **prediction.** Make sure to show what **helps or hurts** the two different birds' **chances of survival.**

The model showing my prediction:

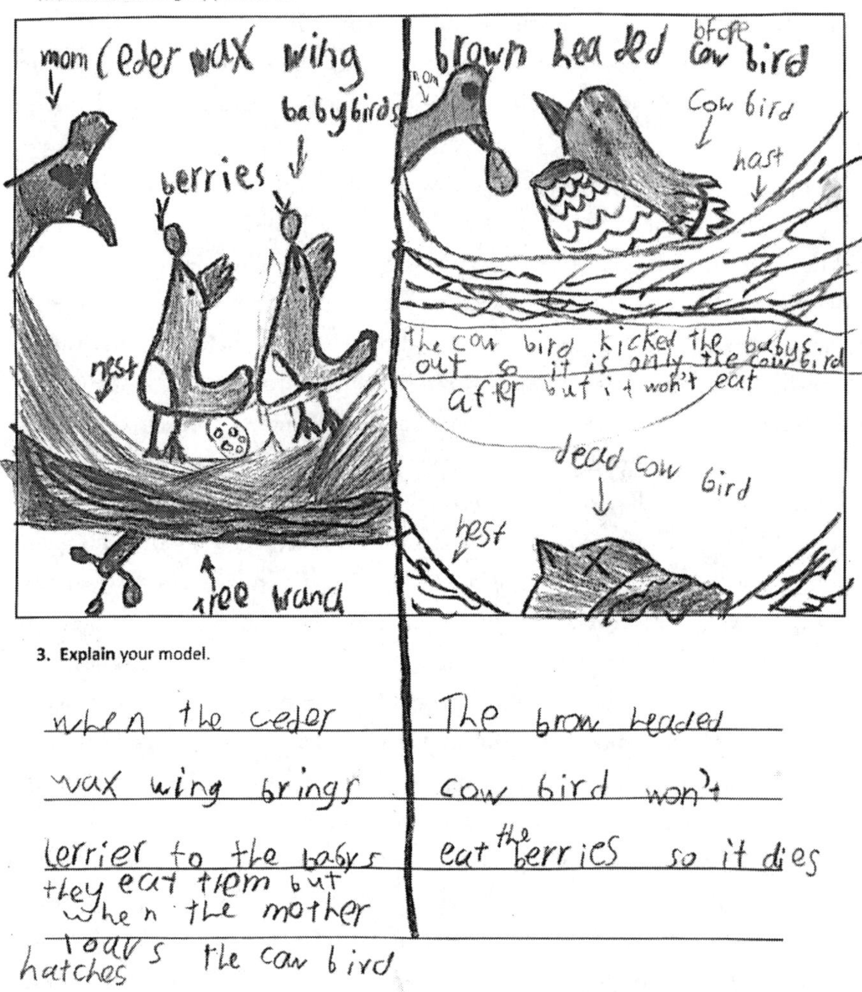

DISCUSSION

Real-world phenomena or problems can be understood as complex systems that require students to use the lens of systems and system models—in other words, systems thinking. In ML-PBL, students are armed with this integral lens through which they learn to apply their ideas to new situations. Across the third-grade units, ML-PBL incorporates systems and system models to engage students in figuring out how components interact with each other when they build models to explain phenomena and solve problems.[6] First, in the Squirrels Unit, they are tasked with creating a model that shows what squirrels need in order to survive and how parts of an environment work together to form a system that allows an organism's (i.e., the squirrel's) needs to be met. They also use a system model to show that when a component in an ecosystem is removed, the system breaks down and some organisms may not survive. This is a complex idea to model, and third-graders are supported to show their thinking through their initial models.

Next, in the Toys Unit, students begin to model a system that has some unseen components. They build on a seen force (their hand pushing a car) to show the same motion from an unseen force (gravity). The students are supported by the teacher to show this new kind of system model using shared class consensus models to consider how to illustrate forces as having strength and directions. In addition, they use the model to explain contrasting systems: one in which a car moves, and the other in which it is at rest. Ms. Kramer also allows the students to struggle with the ideas in small groups, which offers the students emotional safety.

Finally, in the Birds Unit, Ms. Kramer has the students extend all of their systems and system modeling understanding to an unknown hypothetical system. Using what they drew on in the Squirrels and Toys Units, they must develop a model of a hypothetical system—the system that may exist once their bird feeder is placed in the local birds' environment. Students are then able to test their system models after the bird feeder has been placed.

Throughout the school year, Ms. Kramer supports her students in deep learning using crosscutting concepts related to systems thinking, including patterns and cause and effect. As their teacher, she interacts with them in a variety of ways to foster their sustained interaction with real-world phenomena to develop artifacts and think like scientists. She works with the students individually, in small groups, or as a whole class, prodding them to identify components and figure out the relationships among those components.

Systems thinking is a lens that scientists use in their careers, as it plays a critical role in explaining phenomena, solving scientific problems, and proposing solutions to societal issues, such as water quality, global warming, and pandemics. Through systems thinking and immersion in interesting questions, and the practices of investigations, developing models, and engineering design, Ms. Kramer builds a foundation of thinking that the children can use throughout their lives to solve problems.

CHAPTER 7

An Equitable Intervention for Student Science Achievement

KAYLA BARTZ AND I-CHIEN CHEN

It is Tuesday afternoon, and Ms. Tilson is busily preparing her notes. She will be giving directions on having her students construct a model of what happens to squirrels when there is a change in the environment. Reflecting on the last few weeks of lessons in the Squirrels Unit, Ms. Tilson is excited to see how her students—many of whom struggle with reading—have become interested in and excited about learning more about the animals that live right outside their apartments and homes: what they eat, where they live, and what other animals—such as dogs—chase after them. Although she has been a science teacher for many years, Ms. Tilson notes how project-based learning (PBL) has opened up opportunities that traditional science learning materials have often failed to, in the resource-limited classrooms where she has chosen to dedicate her entire professional life as a teacher. As she unlocks the Chromebook cart where the laptops are stored (these are shared among the ninety students in third grade), she smiles to herself, thinking about how PBL has brought a new view of science equity into her class and bridged new intellectual opportunities that her students did not have in the past.

The most rewarding experience Ms. Tilson has had this year is her participation in Multiple Literacies in Project-Based Learning (ML-PBL) and watching the effect on her students. Many of the students in this class are nearly at the bottom of standardized test scores for this age group; however, they have been eager and willing to engage in science activities that have been presented in the ML-PBL unit activities. Ms. Tilson often thinks that this may be due to their experiences in ML-PBL that encourage the drawing of models—these allow struggling readers to learn and acquire different skills that can help them in all of their academic subjects, including science. She believes that these experiences help her students build a passion for science and finds the ML-PBL program valuable because "it is developmental and designed with the third graders in mind." ML-PBL is a comprehensive and engaging teaching and learning program in elementary science—even for students who have learning disabilities, such as ADHD, who still remain focused during their observing, learning, and discussing.

Equity is a major focus of PBL, providing *all students* with experiences that allow them to ask questions, share ideas, collaborate in teams, and build models.[1] In traditional classrooms, when science is taught to third-graders, it is often taught from books and exercises. PBL works to transform classrooms into animated places where science learning is made accessible to everyone as they make sense of the world around them. The principles as substantiated in the intervention are designed to benefit all students, which is especially imperative for children who are in low-income communities and communities with few material resources in their classrooms and schools. As explained in chapter 6 (Ms. Kramer's case), a systems thinking approach grounded in three-dimensional learning emphasizes crosscutting concepts to help students use a scientific lens to conceive big picture ideas. These ideas then enable them to identify, build boundaries around, and understand how components interact with one another.[2] In this case, we show how Ms. Tilson organizes her instruction and how the third-grade students exemplify systems thinking—in their modeling, explanations, and evidence—as shown in the post-unit tests in the Squirrels and Birds Units.

SCAFFOLDING AND ENCOURAGING STUDENTS' USE OF NOTEBOOKS AND LANGUAGE IN THE SQUIRRELS UNIT

During the Squirrels Unit, Ms. Tilson introduces the Driving Question, which focuses on how animals survive and adapt to changes in the environment, asking about their past, present, and future evolution. In lesson 4.4, students are engaging with different texts in groups and making claims to construct arguments about what differences in the environment meant to extinct organisms (Juramaia and the stegosaurus) and current organisms (squirrels). Ms. Tilson hooks students' interest and engages their thinking with the Driving Question for the unit (*Why do I see so many squirrels but can't find any stegosauruses?*), the Driving Question for the lesson (*Which organisms could live in prehistoric environments?*), and the connections between previous lessons. While students are still thinking about the lesson questions, Ms. Tilson circulates to assist students in reading and interpreting their text, helping to identify where difficulties occur in the text and what difficulties they encounter during their reading. She asks students to write their answers in their notebook. Through the scaffolding of the reading materials step-by-step, Ms. Tilson creates opportunities for students to use their own words to express their thinking, knowing, and findings. Moreover, she "breaks things down into smaller segments for the students, so that the task is somewhat more limited in its content but [is] coherent, and I restate it each time." As Ms. Tilson explains, half of her students have learning disabilities, so this segmentation allows the students to stay engaged and present in the activity.

Another opportunity Ms. Tilson gives the students relates to self-reflection. When the students finish the read-aloud stories, she asks them to write in their journals. She explains, "I do not ask them to tell me what the story was about or an individual within the story; instead, I ask them to reflect on the story and what they learned from it. This helps to reinforce the idea of the reading, while also placing it in the student's life experiences, which they then can reinforce in their memory." Throughout the entire lesson, Ms. Tilson also walks around the classroom, back and forth, to ensure that students are writing their thoughts, ideas, observations, and answers in their journal.

Students Asking Questions, Small-Group Sharing, and Collaboration

After completing the readings, students work with other peers who read the same passage to discuss it. In their groups, students need to write in their journals about how animals use their structures to survive. During the small-group discussion, Ms. Tilson also monitors group work and asks the groups questions to help them figure out the answers and the connections between the questions and the readings. Ms. Tilson explains, "I try to teach them decorum in their interactions, not saying to each other that an idea is stupid but rather learning how to talk with one another with respect. When I did that, I found many changes in their attention and ability to describe what they saw." She considers one of her learning successes with her students to be that "all [her] students were able to better express themselves regardless of their reading level, and all had a growing curiosity about science."

Scaffolding Activities and Engaging Students in System Thinking

Ms. Tilson embraces the interactive and immersive aspect of ML-PBL in her classroom. During the Squirrels Unit, she works to get the students to think outside of the box and integrate what they are learning during their "science block" into other aspects of their lives. As mentioned in previous chapters (see especially chapters 4 [Ms. Lane's case] and 6 [Ms. Kramer's case]), one of the main components of ML-PBL is literacy, which Ms. Tilson defines as "reading, writing, and interpreting passages and data."

Ms. Tilson's class has below-average reading scores: with this in mind, she has her students not only read, observe, and discuss the different characteristics of squirrels and what they need for survival but has them engage in an activity that tasks them to use their knowledge on squirrels and literacy. Ms. Tilson tells the students, "Today, in gym class, you are all going to jump like squirrels." "How are we going to do that?" Georgie wonders. Ms. Tilson looks around the room and asks, "Well how do squirrels jump?" Anna responds, "With their legs!" Ms. Tilson asks, "What about their legs?" William then mentions that squirrels use their claws and back legs "to jump into trees and run real fast!" Ms. Tilson smiles at the class: "Exactly! So, what I want you all to do is, during gym, you are going to mark a starting position on the floor and then jump as far as you can. Mark where you land and measure how far away you are from the starting point. Write down your length and bring it back to me. I have talked with your gym teachers, and they will help and go over the instructions again. Any questions?"

Ms. Tilson's students immerse themselves in the Squirrels Unit not simply by reading about squirrels or merely observing them but by putting themselves in the squirrel's "shoes" and making connections with other disciplines—which is supported by systems thinking. Systems thinking supports the students in understanding the different aspects of the squirrel that help with their survival. In addition, once the students record the length of their jumps, they bring these measurements back to Ms. Tilson's class and now have their own data—strengthening their math, reading, interpretation, and discussion of the varying skills.

One of the questions in the Squirrels Unit assessment asks, "How do people learn about squirrels and their changing habitats?", while another asks, "How do you think learning about squirrels and their habitats can help people?" The lesson unit that follows, which includes observations and writing in their notebooks, helps the students understand how data are collected and allows them to think like a scientist, using the same kinds of tools and skills scientists use to collect information on various habitats and animals. Having an activity that crosses over into other classes and uses multiple skills is something Ms. Tilson finds "powerful." She describes the activity as "taking something out of the box and seeing something in a totally different domain . . . It is all connected. Learning is connected. And showing the kids how it was connected was powerful."

The ML-PBL materials are designed to have students use crosscutting concepts across sequential units. Teachers help students develop a deep understanding of cause-and-effect relationships. Ms. Tilson explains, "If children can learn to make interconnections visible or draw a causal graph to show the patterns, they are better able to understand the complex system and its effect on the behavior on animals' survival." This process provides a context for teachers to transform the classroom into a place of observing, discovering, investigating, and discussing the phenomenon—thus linking children's science learning to real-world events.

STUDENTS' PERFORMANCE AND SQUIRRELS UNIT ASSESSMENT

The Squirrels Unit is the first unit that students experience that is designed to assess students' science understanding about survival, adaptation, and ecosystem dynamics. In this unit, they are asked a series of questions related to squirrels' body features, survival, adaptations, and ecosystem changes. "Adaptation" and "change in the environment causes change" are two disciplinary core ideas (DCIs), along with the crosscutting concepts (CCCs) of "Structure and Function" and "Systems and System Models" in this unit. The Driving Question of this unit is: *Why do I see so many squirrels but can't find any stegosauruses?* To show how Ms. Tilson's class responded to the Squirrels Unit, we provide examples from the unit assessments.

Before and After the Squirrels Unit Assessment: Student Examples

Student 1: Sharon. Figure 7.1 shows a model drawn by Sharon, who is a struggling reader. The post-test assessment asks the students to draw a model that describes "what happens to the squirrel's survival and clearly states or shows

FIGURE 7.1 Sharon's model of squirrel survival

the relationship between having no trees with what happens to the squirrel." Sharon's drawing uses words, labels, and pictures to describe what happens to a squirrel when all the trees are cut down. Her model demonstrates her understanding that the squirrels would not only lose their home and food source but will become vulnerable to predators, as depicted by the owl. Sharon writes, "The squirrels have nowhere to hide or a place to be safe and warm."

Concerning adaptation, students are asked how the squirrels will react when their habitat changes. In response, Sharon writes, "If the habitat changes, some animals may die because they won't have food or water. Another idea of what might happen is the squirrel if you chop down all the trees, they won't have a home but maybe they can find another home." This answer indicates that Sharon understands there are multiple effects that can result from cutting down the trees, but she does not give a detailed explanation of how or why there is no food or shelter for the squirrels. Sharon demonstrates that she understands the importance of the trees in the squirrels' habitat and that if their environment changes dramatically, the squirrels may be forced to move away and find another home. The connection between her drawing and writing illustrates Sharon's cognition of the concepts and relationships between aspects in a system using diagrams, which is a crucial skill in model development.

Regarding the dynamics of the ecosystem, the students are asked, "After millions of years, what are possible changes you might see in Eastern Gray Squirrels that survived?" Sharon writes, "After millions of years in a different habitat organisms that live there will change by because if it wasn't no trees his tail will get small and he can get skinny and he can eat bugs off the ground and different claw types of claws." She shows that she understands the importance of the differing functions of each part of the squirrel's body and that, for the squirrel to survive in the same place for millions of years, they must adapt, change, and evolve along with the environment around them.

Student 2: Frankford. Frankford is very behind in his reading comprehension compared to his peers; however, this does not appear to hinder his ability to understand the disciplinary core ideas of adaptation and the scientific practice of modeling, as illustrated in his model and explanation (see figure 7.2). He writes, "After millions of years in a different habitat, organisms that live there will change by the squirrel's powerful hind legs. Getting faster." Frankford thus shows he understands the importance of the function of the different physical parts of the body on the squirrel and what can change in the squirrel body regarding functions that will help the squirrel survive.

FIGURE 7.2 Frankford's model of squirrel adaptation

Student 3: Melissa. Melissa is also far behind her peers in reading comprehension; however, she is able to understand the modeling and adaptation that is prominent throughout this unit. She writes, "I think the Eastern Gray squirrels survive because of their sharp claws scare off predators with the claws and use them to climb trees and eat." Melissa demonstrates her understanding of the multifunctional nature of a squirrel's claws and their importance to survival. She understands that there is a connection between the ability of the squirrels to survive in how they use their claws for food and defense, which is an illustration of her developing systems thinking.

Student 4: Barman. Barman has above-average reading comprehension. Importantly, he uses multiple concepts in the same drawing to express his understanding and solutions for squirrels to survive. He draws the different predators that the squirrel can no longer hide from (fox), and shows that, with no homes to hide in or available food, the squirrels will get sick; moreover, different animals may move to the forest, causing the squirrels to leave. However, Barman's drawing also includes bushes, showing that new and different habitats may pop up in place of the trees. Barman demonstrates his understanding that the environment is all about change, and that change affects not just one element in a specific region or habitat, but many elements—plants and animals alike. In other words, he is demonstrating his understanding of the connections between organisms and their environment. In response to the question asking students, "How do you think learning about squirrels and their environment can help people?" Barman writes, "Learning about squirrels and their habitats can help people by eating up all the little critters that the trees have so we could have more oxygen." Here, Barman is demonstrating an understanding that squirrels and their habitat are not only important for the animal itself but for everyone, when he mentions that the squirrels' habitat (trees) supply oxygen to humans. Barman recognizes the connection between squirrels' food source and home with potential human food sources, and how both squirrels and people would be affected by a lack of trees in the environment.

OBSERVING AND IDENTIFYING DIFFERENCES BETWEEN BIRDS

In the Birds Unit, the Driving Question asks the students to think about: *How can we help the birds near our school grow up and thrive?* Students are tasked with recognizing and identifying different characteristics and traits that allow the birds to survive, as well as traits that are adaptive due to the environment versus those that are genetically predisposed. Once again, Ms. Tilson, guided by the ML-PBL materials, encourages her students to make observations, collaborate, and get excited about science. She tells the class, "Today, we are going to go outside! But first each of you need to pick a partner." Once the partners are decided, each pair is given a pair of binoculars. We are going to be observing the different birds we see outside. So, follow me." The students follow Ms. Tilson outside and toward the trees. "Now, I want you and your partner to try and spot and identify as many birds as you can. Discuss with one another the bird's traits and why you think it is that type of bird. Questions?"

The students spread a little farther apart to start looking for birds. They use binoculars to look up at the branches of the trees and surrounding skies. "Oh, I think I see a cardinal," says Anna. "I see a turkey vulture!" shouts Billie. "I see an eagle," yells Georgie, not to be outdone. The other students giggle and continue to search the trees and skies to find the biggest or rarest bird. Ms. Tilson encourages the students to continue looking and talking to one another about what they see. Here, Ms. Tilson is immersing the students in the unit not just by reading and writing about birds but actually observing the birds in their natural habitat. She encourages them to think about the different species of birds and what makes them distinct. Once the students are back in the classroom, Ms. Tilson asks them, "Please describe the different birds you saw based on the birds' feathers, beak, and feet. Try to infer what you thought and what the birds were doing and why the birds were doing that, such as foraging for food and/or building a nest." During the unit, the students build a birdhouse and/or a bird feeder. However, Ms. Tilson does not simply give her students a design to follow, but instead asks them questions. She reminds the students that "different birds have different needs, so their houses would need to be different from one another." She indicates the varying materials from which the students must choose, such as toilet paper rolls, wax from crayons, and plastic water bottles. She has them decide which materials to use, the dimensions (vertically and horizontally), and any other considerations based on what is best for certain types of birds. This encourages the students to start thinking on their own, asking questions and making decisions based on their knowledge and experiences.

STUDENTS' PERFORMANCE AND THE BIRDS UNIT ASSESSMENT

In Ms. Tilson's classroom, the Birds Unit is being taught near the end of the semester. It was designed to help students understand that organisms have characteristics—including traits, behaviors, and life cycles—that result from interactions with the environment and genetic material passed through generation. In this unit's post-assessment, students are asked a series of questions related to two birds and their traits, behaviors, and life cycles. Here, "Environmental and genetic factors influence an organism's characteristics," "Certain characteristics/traits allow success," and "The environment influences traits" are three DCIs, along with four CCCs including "Patterns," "Cause and Effect," "Structure and Function," and "Systems and System Models."

Student 1: Dawn. Dawn is below average on reading comprehension but scores very high on understanding the modeling in the Birds Unit. In the assessment, students are asked to make a prediction about: "What will happen when [a] cedar waxwing mother brings food to the chicks?" and to draw a model to show their prediction. Dawn writes, "I think the cedar waxwing mother will feed the brown-headed cowbird too and her baby birds."

Dawn is asked, "Will the brown-headed cowbirds look and behave the same as the cedar waxwings?" and "Will each of the cedar waxwing chicks grow up to look and behave exactly the same as one another?" In response, she writes "No, because the brown-headed cowbird and the cedar waxwing has different traits, colors, foods, and different parents," and "They are not exactly the same, because they are different species. When they grow, they will be different birds."

Dawn illustrates her understanding about different species, different traits, behaviors and life cycles. Her model shows the cedar waxwing mother bringing a strawberry to feed the chicks. Cedar waxwings are known to eat fruits and berries, while the brown-headed cowbird is known to eat insects, grasshoppers, and seeds. Dawn understands that, as the mother is a different species of bird, she will not bring to the nest the kinds of food a brown-headed cowbird would normally eat; however, since it is in her nature to feed the chicks, she will feed the cowbirds what she would feed her own. When asked whether the two types of birds would look and behave the same, Dawn answers, "No," and comments on their physical appearance, traits, foods, and genetics—in other words, showing her understanding that the chicks are a different species from one another.

To once again get the students thinking like scientists, the assessment tasks them to think about what scientists do with regard to observing and helping birds. Dawn writes, "The scientists figure out how to help birds survive." Here, she is demonstrating that scientific work can help birds survive. She shows that having a better understanding of how birds survive and thrive in the wild by observing what they eat, their traits, and their habitats will enable scientists to help birds. This illustrates that she—along with her classmates—is beginning to understand that to help an animal, one cannot assume there is a catch-all solution, or one thing to do, as it depends on the animal and the species.

Finally, students are asked, "Why is it important for people to know about how animals survive and thrive?" This question is aimed at getting the students to once again connect what they are learning in class to their lives and those of others. Dawn writes, "It is important because what happen to bird will happen to us." Here, she is connecting what may happen to a bird who is no longer being taken care of by his own species/mother to this happening to a person who may not be raised by his or her own parents. In her response, Dawn shows her understanding that it is important to acknowledge similarities among individuals, but also to recognize their differences as these must be taken into account—not only for birds but for people as well. This question gets at one of the goals of ML-PBL, which is making the lessons more meaningful and impactful by connecting their experiences to the lessons learned in class.

Student 2: Carol. In her model, Carol illustrates the cedar waxwing mother giving all of the chicks in the nest fruit and berries to eat (figure 7.3). She draws the brown-headed cowbird differently from the other birds, indicating an understanding that the two species of birds differ in appearance.

Carol is asked, "Will the brown-headed cowbirds look and behave the same as the cedar waxwings?" and "Will each of the cedar waxwing chicks grow up to look and behave exactly the same as one another?" She writes, "No, I don't think that the Brown-headed Birds are going to be the same because they have different traits, and they might live somewhere else" and

"No, because every bird has a different behavior because each Cedar Waxwing baby has a unique behavior." Here, Carol is demonstrating her understanding that certain animals share specific characteristics but that each individual bird is unique and distinct from one another.

FIGURE 7.3 Carol's model of bird survival

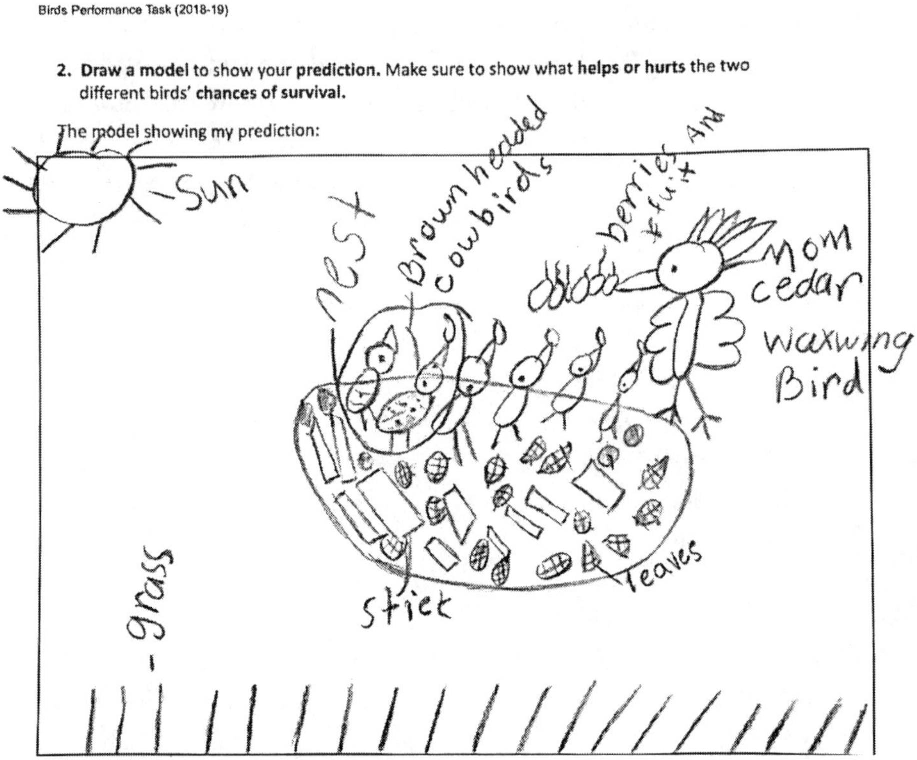
Birds Performance Task (2018-19)
2. Draw a model to show your prediction. Make sure to show what helps or hurts the two different birds' chances of survival.
The model showing my prediction:
Sun
nest
Brown headed cowbirds
berries And fruit
Mom cedar waxwing Bird
grass
stick
leaves

Student 3: Mara. Mara also draws a mother bird feeding the chicks in her nest. Mara describes her model by writing, "So the mother bird is feeding the hatchlings and the babies mouths' open for some food." Here, unlike in the other students' models, Mara is describing the actual feeding process, which demonstrates how reliant the hatchlings are on the mother bird for their survival.

Mara's response regarding whether the two species of hatchlings will look and behave the same is very similar to the students' examples above: "No, because they don't sound the same, look different, and different traits and they eat different foods." Here, she exhibits her understanding that the two species of birds have different appearances, make different sounds, and require varying food sources.

When asked if the chicks that are the same species (cedar waxwing) will all be the same, Mara writes, "No because I have another brother and three sisters that do not look like me and because some of them are boys." By making this connection with her family, Mara demonstrates the importance of each individual animal's uniqueness despite sharing the same genetics. Mara shows that she understands that all birds are different based on their traits, characteristics, appearance, and the food they eat. In addition, she shows that, not only are their genetic characteristics important, but the chicks are also dependent on the mother for survival. Finally, Mara connects the bird's unique characteristics by using her own family to demonstrate that even individuals with the same genes will look and act differently from one another.

DISCUSSION

In this case, we see how Ms. Tilson not only used the ML-PBL curriculum but was fluid in her use of it and was able to adapt it to meet the needs of her students. As mentioned earlier, a high percentage of her students struggled with reading. She therefore scaffolded her lessons and read aloud to the class to level the playing field for all students. She wanted to ensure that each student had an opportunity to learn, understand, and contribute to the conversation. Ms. Tilson reflected,

> The hardest thing was the completion of responding to writing prompts. It is something about writing that intimidates children who are struggling with literacy skills. And that remains a problem. However, I saw growth in their reading skills because of all that we were doing. I think ML-PBL had a huge part to play in that because it was a venue they enjoyed. They liked it. And so they were motivated, simply because it was very gratifying for the children to be able to participate. And kids were looking forward to what is next, continually asking what was next and referring to previous lessons.

To help students overcome this fear of reading and writing, Ms. Tilson gave them notebooks in which they were instructed to write their thoughts and ideas. She connected this with the students' English language arts block and their vocabulary lessons, which they then used to go back and rewrite previous entries using new vocabulary words. She wanted the students to be able to make connections across not only the ML-PBL units but other subjects as well. This method allowed her students to be able to make connections and draw models of cause and effect, which demonstrates systems thinking.

In Ms. Tilson, we see a teacher who is passionate about becoming a facilitator for student learning. She encouraged her students to become "authentic learners" by showing them how to ask questions and where to find answers. She also encouraged students to collaborate with one another, including sharing ideas in a respectful way and asking each other questions. Ms. Tilson shared the following example:

> [I had] a kid with low reading skills—pre-primary level, he was reading at a kindergarten level. He was going around showing the other kids [how to do an activity] and then the other students started asking him how he did that. And he was like, "All you have to do is . . . " And then watching them go off and teach each other. Priceless. It was priceless. It was amazing to hear them engage all twenty-nine kids working their butts off and being amazed by their discoveries. Quiet kids who are shy who normally would not speak, talking about being excited, enjoying in-the-moment learning.

The most important point of this case study is to demonstrate that ML-PBL is for all students.[3] This particular class and their post-test are a tribute to not only Ms. Tilson's effort and dedication to her students, but to all the ML-PBL units, activities, and experiences. A Robert Frost quotation might well describe Ms. Tilson's approach to teaching: "I am not a teacher, but an awakener." She moved away from being the fountain of all knowledge toward being a teacher who encouraged her students to seek their own questions and answers and realize there is always more to learn and discover. Ms. Tilson awoke their curiosity and gave them the tools to explore the world around them using scientific practices, where they could reflect on their work and collaborate with others.

CHAPTER 8

Integrating ML-PBL Science with English Language Arts and Literacy

SUSAN CODERE

> It was the day before spring break, and I was just trying to finish a unit. And I told them we were going to have all-day science. It was going to be science all day. And I had cheering! They were so excited!
>
> —MS. HEGG

At the end of the 2017–2018 school year, Ms. Hegg, a teacher in a small rural school, wished that she had found a way to better incorporate Michigan's new science standards into her curricular plan for that year. This had been her fourth year teaching third-grade science, and though she tried to teach it differently every year, she always felt something was missing. Later that summer, she was thrilled to learn that her district had been assigned to implement Multiple Literacies in Project-Based Learning (ML-PBL) at the third-grade level. With encouragement from her principal, Ms. Hegg began in earnest to learn what she could about the ML-PBL science resources, the thinking that would be promoted, and the instructional changes she would make to better prepare her students for succeeding in science. She set goals for the year—for herself as well as for her students—and began to identify strategies for reworking the focus of her literacy and language arts instruction to leverage opportunities for developing literacy practices while teaching science. She was excited to enact this new approach in her fifth year of teaching third-grade science, and first year enacting ML-PBL practices.

The case follows Ms. Hegg through four ML-PBL units as she transitions from "sure she is not doing justice to science standards" to "confident that she is supporting her students in meeting science and literacy standards."[1] By using ML-PBL units to provide a larger context and routines for daily instruction and adapting literacy lessons to provide a foundation for science learning, Ms. Hegg was able to generate and sustain excitement for learning across content areas. Focusing on features of ML-PBL lessons that are designed to formatively assess students' progress, Ms. Hegg found ways to use the project-based learning (PBL) science model to integrate science and English language arts (ELA)/literacy instruction. By beginning with one hour each day devoted to science instruction, she was able to carry the science context throughout most days and watch her students become drivers of their own learning and of their ability to showcase what they had learned. She shared, "I was looking for the one piece that I've been missing, and I really believe this is it. I really love how it's going, and I was excited to try it."

Ms. Hegg is fortunate to work in a district whose culture is supportive of teacher agency and shared leadership. With only one teacher per grade level in each of two elementary schools in the district, Ms. Hegg and her colleagues are able to make decisions about their professional learning (PL) experiences. After hearing a description of the PL support for integrating science and literacy instruction in ML-PBL, Ms. Hegg and her principal arranged for their literacy coach (a regional literacy consultant) to work with the district's two third-grade teachers to plan for a more integrated approach to learning science and to develop a plan for full integration of science and literacy. Together, they developed a framework for enacting the ML-PBL units and extending the science contexts throughout the day.

As the semester began, Ms. Hegg focused on enacting the science lessons as designed, while developing plans for further supporting students' science learning during the portions of the day devoted to ELA/literacy and addressing as many literacy standards as possible. Here, her intention was to plan ahead for science class and then adjust her ELA instruction to better align with and extend her students' science learning. She began the year by introducing science notebooks as an important tool that her students, as scientists, would use throughout the year. Early in the first unit (the Squirrels Unit), she read *Notable Notebooks: Scientists and Their Writings* to expose her students to the kinds of observational notes, drawings, and plans scientists from different time periods used as they conducted investigations to make sense of their worlds.[2] She wanted to help her students adopt the idea that "We are scientists here." She referred back to this text often during the year as students recorded observations and drafted initial models in their science notebooks as part of their ML-PBL lessons.

To strengthen her reading and writing instruction, Ms. Hegg paid close attention to the focus of the science lessons, considered what she could extend to meet literacy standards, and identified the PBL and lesson features she was most comfortable carrying through to the rest of her day.[3] She began with the *discourse moves*—features highlighted in each science lesson. She credited these as helping students articulate their thinking in preparation for writing about what they have experienced (in observations, investigations, or in reading), while also strengthening their speaking and listening skills throughout all subject area instruction. Ms. Hegg described her support for using the discourse moves across content areas and their importance in ELA instruction:

> I really have big aspirations for my students in writing and in reading to use accountable talk. That's really going well, and I especially like that we use discourse moves across math and reading and writing. I can redo a lot of my reading and writing curriculum around what we have here in science to make it all fit and flow. I would say my reading instruction has enhanced my science instruction because I spend a lot of time on speaking and listening. When my students presented their [interconnections among organisms] findings the other day, they were genuinely interested to know that they had the same organism as somebody else. They listened carefully, planning ahead to say something new or different [as if thinking], "This is really important and I'm not going to say the same thing that someone else just said. I'm going to add and say something else." I saw this happening often. It was exciting.

ENHANCING SCIENCE LEARNING BY ADDING SCIENCE-RELATED LITERACY EXPERIENCES

The literacy program Ms. Hegg used as a resource for planning ELA/literacy instruction suggests daily shared reading, interactive read-alouds, and differentiated instruction experiences.[4] Ms. Hegg reviewed the read-alouds and shared readings in the literacy program to identify the opportunities they provided for supporting ELA standards—opportunities she would need to replicate as she selected science-related replacement texts. The texts Ms. Hegg chose for the read-alouds were mostly well above grade level to build students' language and vocabulary knowledge, world knowledge, and inferential thinking. She also added texts to fortify the *interest and engagement* already generated in the Squirrels Unit, while modeling appropriate fluency (accuracy, automaticity, and prosody) in reading, discussing character traits, authors' and characters' points of view, and analyzing the use of illustrations. In addition, the texts offered examples for noticing how authors use nouns (regular, plural, and abstract).

To provide opportunities for her third-grade students to hear, think about, and use language that would support their thinking in three of the four ML-PBL science units, Ms. Hegg chose *What Is a Biome?* for a read-aloud.[5] Including this text at the beginning of the school year provided opportunities for building familiarity with life- and earth-science words and common background knowledge on which students could build as they considered questions throughout the Squirrels, Birds, and Plants units. The text offered opportunities to discuss child-friendly explanations of words, encouraging students to say the words aloud—activities that might build students' confidence in using these words as they talk about what they are learning in science. Ms. Hegg selected additional read-alouds and shared reading articles to prompt asking questions and making connections with their science investigations.[6]

During the interactive read-alouds, students learned words, but also learned new ideas and acquired new ways to name those ideas. They provided great opportunities for students to ask questions during reading, many of which were added to the Squirrels Unit Driving Question Board (DQB). The text offered a beginning look at informational text structures and features (e.g., bolded headings, captions to support understanding of pictures and diagrams, and representations such as a circular timeline to show cycles with a sequence of events that repeat)—all recorded on a text structure anchor chart that would grow as students read more informational texts and noted text structures and features. Ms. Hegg found herself going back to pages of this text throughout the year as warranted by student questions and comments placed on the Driving Question Board.

In addition to informational texts, Ms. Hegg read aloud the novel *Flora and Ulysses: The Illuminated Adventures*, which highlights outstanding characterizations and fun misadventures. Told in prose with graphic novel pages, the text provided opportunities for discussing features of graphic novels and fantasy.[7] And since she had started the year with another text by the same author (Kate

DiCamillo), reading *Flora and Ulysses* provided opportunities for an author study of sorts.[8] As Ms. Hegg explained, "It is a silly story with not much science in it, but it did fuel the students' interest in squirrels, and during the read-aloud sessions, students wondered [asked questions] that related to the Squirrel[s] Unit and which they placed on the DQB."

Finally, Ms. Hegg incorporated grammar, seeking unusual bridges between science and ELA and leveraging her knowledge that many elements of grammar are addressed in science texts. Ms. Hegg explained that she would choose mentor sentences from texts she had already read aloud during science (from an ML-PBL science lesson, for example) and then use them again later in the day in two main ways: modeling *Patterns of Power*, as shared by Jeff Anderson, and in scrambled sentences, as suggested in the Bookworms resources.[9] At this beginning stage of third grade, Ms. Hegg focused on finding examples of pronoun use and pronoun–antecedent agreement, descriptive language, and literal and non-literal meanings. She acknowledged her surprise that her students loved unscrambling sentences—a practice she thought they might not find interesting—and she marveled each time they were excited to recognize the mentor sentences when they revisited the texts in later instruction.

FINE-TUNING THE INTEGRATION PLAN—HIGHLIGHTING EQUITY, PERSEVERANCE, AND RISK-TAKING AND EXTENDING TO SOCIAL STUDIES AND MATH

Ms. Hegg fine-tuned ELA and science integration by reflecting on the evidence of what was working. She continued to build on the enthusiasm engendered by the science units and brought in texts, student writing and grammar, and equity topics that had high interest. She shared that her students loved the Toys Unit—the engagement, building and redesigning toys, and learning about engineers. They were really invested in figuring out the Driving Question, *How can we design fun moving toys that any kid can build?* She noted again that because of this engagement, science continued to provide an on-ramp to ELA: "There was so much interaction the whole time. And students quickly learned that every time there was a reading, they knew there was a piece that they could not figure out until they learned more about it. They knew the reading was going to help them expand their thinking and come up with new questions. But particularly the Lonnie Johnson text—they loved that story. They really engaged with that text."

After about two weeks of considering "How can we make toys that move?"—generating questions, interviewing kindergarten students, describing the pattern of motion and forces that cause toys to begin moving, building and modeling a prototype toy to redesign—Ms. Hegg's students were ready to learn about the engineering design process. Just days before Martin Luther King, Jr., Day, they read "From Water Squirter to Super Soaker: How Lonnie Johnson Changed the Water Games," an interactive read-aloud text included in the Toys Unit. The story introduces students to Lonnie Johnson, a NASA scientist whose win in a school science fair was not acknowledged because he was Black. The story describes Dr. Johnson's love of science and making things, and also describes the engineering processes in which he engaged. Ms. Hegg's students loved this story, and the videos, interviews, and later interactive read-aloud of *Whoosh!: Lonnie Johnson's Super Soaking Stream of Inventions.*[10] They considered similarities and differences in the different informational texts they read to learn about Lonnie Johnson and his experiences. Ms. Hegg shared her class's reaction to the readings in the unit: "We are predominantly white in our district. The students felt the injustice in what happened to Lonnie Johnson. I was able to actually take that energy and interest level and grow other parts of my literacy time. I shared some other stories for MLK Day—stories that sometimes fell flat in other years because the students didn't relate to them. This year, they were engaged and interested."[11] The Lonnie Johnson story was the first science unit piece Ms. Hegg carried through the day, as she recounted in her third interview: "That Lonnie Johnson text changed a lot. What my students did with that story helped me begin integrating better in other areas. I realized I could stretch parts of the science lesson right through reading. But I could do that in writing as well. That really changed things for us."

As she planned for integrating science and literacy in the Toys Unit, Ms. Hegg looked more closely at the interactive read-alouds and shared readings featured in the science unit to identify those she would carry into her literacy time. She also looked for texts to extend the engineering focus of the unit. She found the Classroom Library Connections resource provided as a part of the ML-PBL unit to be a great source for investigating additional texts to use in her reading instruction.[12] Ms. Hegg replaced some of her planned reading texts with three interactive read-alouds to extend students' thinking about engineers and engineering design. She selected sentences from these texts to use in grammar and writing instruction and found that they offered many examples of comparative and superlative adjectives and adverbs, conjunctions, and simple, compound, and complex sentences. In addition to reading for enjoyment and with a great deal to notice and wonder (thus adding to the Driving Question Board), these texts helped her students realize that many successful inventors experience failure. To build self-esteem and to help students keep imagining possibilities, Ms. Hegg selected texts that focused on *making mistakes and learning from them*. She worked to build a community where students felt *safe to take risks*. She noticed that her students who struggled with or were uncertain in math began asking questions and collaborating in science and that their comfort with risk-taking carried over into their math lessons. They became more comfortable with trying, making mistakes, and persevering to find an explanation or to solve a problem in mathematics.

MOVING FROM LITERACY IN SCIENCE AND SCIENCE IN LITERACY TO SEAMLESS INTEGRATION

Ms. Hegg chose to focus her writing instruction on research report writing as she planned for the Birds Unit Driving Question: *How can we help the birds near our school grow up and thrive?* She reviewed recommended titles for texts to support students in figuring out more about the birds they were studying and for meeting Common Core State Standards (CCSS) for Literacy. Her students spent a great deal of time using computers to learn about birds. They loved the "All About Birds" website sponsored by the Cornell Lab of Ornithology and featured in the Birds Unit, and began to gather information to share what they learned about their chosen birds.[13] The two trade books—*Beaks!* and *Four Feet, Two Sandals*—already included in the Birds Unit provided opportunities for addressing literacy and social studies goals.[14] From the Classroom Library list, Ms. Hegg selected four texts to read aloud, and at the recommendation of colleagues during the PL session for the Birds Unit, she added a listening text.[15] Ms. Hegg shared that when she chooses to use a book from her literacy resource recommendations, she tries the follow-up writing and reflection lessons and sometimes comes back to the book again later to address different standards or to practice additional comprehension skills. She noted the variety of ways she uses the extension texts:

> Sometimes I use the science literacy piece (from the unit or one I choose) as a transition from science to math or reading lessons; sometimes I start with a story and then move to science and science ideas. Sometimes, after I have used

> the text to talk about science for a few times, I use it again for grammar or other skill work, but only after the science "is washed out of it" and we look at it for a different purpose.

Ms. Hegg shared that she began the Birds Unit by reading *The Boy Who Drew Birds: The Story of John James Audubon* as a way to introduce the Audubon website and to consider how one's love of something as a child can continue to represent something important in their life.[16] She helped her students see that Audubon's love of birds has become an enormous organization. She followed by revisiting *Notable Notebooks: Scientists and Their Writings* as a reminder that scientists keep journals—drawing birds and sketches, recording field notes, and planning investigations—just like the students were doing. Her students especially loved the *Beaks!* text and wanted to do more with it. They had a number of questions and wanted to take the examples in the book and visit the Cornell website to find answers to their questions. They also wanted to categorize the birds by beaks and other structures as they categorized questions on the Driving Question Board. Ms. Hegg extended the excitement with *Best Beak in Boonaroo Bay,* a story loaded with information about specialized structures and functions set in a contest to see whose beak is the best.[17]

Ms. Hegg relayed her appreciation for a number of ML-PBL lesson features using examples from the Birds Unit, including her expanded use of the Driving Question Board during read-alouds. She reflected on her experiences with this new way of teaching:

> Students liked being able to ask questions and choosing to look for answers to them. In the Toy[s] Unit, and especially in the Bird[s] Unit, because they spent so much time on the computers, I really started having students add to the DQB and work to find answers to their questions. Asking questions during read-alouds carried over to social studies where they would sometimes ask me questions that I really didn't know the answer to and had to figure out. Since we used a DQB in science, I started using one in social studies also. And the Unit 3 text, *Four Feet, Two Sandals* offered a great connection with the read-alouds I use in social studies. Students' questions centered on reasons for migration/emigration for birds and for people.

Ms. Hegg acknowledged that she appreciated the different ways the ML-PBL lessons are designed to help surface the big ideas, especially the opportunities at the end of each Learning Set for going back to think about what they learned, to *identify the big takeaway for the Learning Set.* She explained her thinking when asked about the progression in students' figuring out phenomena: "I printed out those individual questions so we had that progression of our learning. I felt like I always needed to come back to that: 'And today's the day to answer the big question.' They liked reflecting on and summarizing what we learned; it really helped." By the end of the Birds Unit, Ms. Hegg described what she looked for as evidence of learning in science:

> When I think of assessment now, I think about the integration piece. I look to see whether my students can take what they are learning in science and show that they can use it in their informational writing—that they can write in response, not only to what they/we read, but to what they do and learn in science. Sometimes this kind of response is included in the science lessons, often the transfer is evidenced in the writing we do in response to the read-alouds chosen to enhance both science and literacy.

PLANNING FOR A SHORTENED UNIT

Like many teachers in their first year of ML-PBL implementation, Ms. Hegg found that she had less time than she hoped for teaching the Plants Unit, which centered on the Driving Question, *How can we plan gardens in our community to grow plants for food?* Due to time limits, Ms. Hegg planned differently for read-aloud titles. She used the two texts in the unit, *In the Garden with Dr. Carver* and *No Monkeys, No Chocolate.*[18] She also provided background knowledge about gardening for those students who might not have gardens at home by beginning the new unit with *How Groundhog's Garden Grew.*[19] She first read it for enjoyment in reading time, even though the focus in science was still on birds; she also used it as an opportunity to highlight the author's craft (including word choice, imagery, tone, repetition, and point of view). Here, she ignored the rich life-cycle drawings throughout the book; however, later, when the science lessons called for modeling the life cycle of the mung bean, she revisited the text and had the students describe the different life cycles in the illustrations: "I thought about building background knowledge, pulled books I used in second grade, and read plant stories as an immersion unit because we were so late in the year. I read some of the stories aloud every day. And then when we started the Plant[s] Unit lessons, they had some base for it. The groundhog text, *How Groundhog's Garden Grew,* was great. When we started with the mung bean life cycle, they had some buy-in."

As an additional read-aloud, Ms. Hegg chose *Miss Maple's Seeds*, a wonderful fantasy full of fantastic art. Not only did this text prompt connections to the questions asked and lessons learned in *In the Garden with Dr. Carver*, it also laid the foundation for considering that, to write this fun fantasy with make-believe characters, the author had to do extensive research. As Ms. Hegg explains, "We went back through the book and pulled out all the science she had to know to write the book. They learned that a nonfiction author has to understand the content. Even though the book is categorized as a fantasy and included a lot that is not factual, there is still a lot of science in it."

REFLECTION ON TEACHING AND LEARNING

As the school year ended, Ms. Hegg reflected on her first year enacting ML-PBL and her newly designed instructional day. "I felt like I was a science teacher again . . . At first, it was beyond me because I was so steeped in second-grade science prior to that. We didn't have a good science program, and I didn't have a lot of familiarity with the new grade 3 standards. But with ML-PBL, I finally felt like a science teacher again this year." She shared that the strength of ML-PBL—the units, the PL, students learning to ask questions and to make sense of phenomena—was what allowed for the richness of the extensions and the solid foundation for literacy learning.

Her comments focused mainly on her students and their ability to think like scientists: all outcomes she knew were possible if she found a way to fully support both literacy and science instruction: "I think the students took more ownership towards the end of the year and really spent more time asking the questions and designing their own learning path, which was already designed for them, but they didn't know it. The questions they asked, we usually addressed—almost every time." She also found that they "read differently because they were reading and writing for more of a purpose . . . they had a reason to do what they were doing." She appreciated how "the ML-PBL units provided students with support," in the form of graphic organizers, templates for recording data and thinking, and opportunities to write claims and support them with evidence. Ms. Hegg noted that these scaffolds supported the students in learning how to interpret charts and graphs, and in voicing and responding to their observations. She explained:

They apply what they are learning and they recognize what they are doing as science. I was reading aloud . . . and asked, "What do you notice?" One of my students said, "There are a lot of science words in here." It was a story about a sea creature . . . and I was thinking words having to do with the creature, like "exoskeleton." And he said, "No." The words he noticed were "discuss" and "determine"—words important for sensemaking. The science words that my kids know because of this program are the science words that describe what they do to make sense of phenomena—words that are going to turn them into scientists. At that moment, it was really clear to me that these kids are scientists: they can think like scientists. I think this whole wonderful thing about the project is not learning about plants or learning about birds, it's learning how to think in the assigned context. And they have it.

DISCUSSION

In the name of integration, science topics are often forwarded through literacy, using textbooks or other non-fiction texts as the science lessons. Recent reforms, such as the Next Generation Science Standards (NGSS), call for moving away from textbooks to engaging students in science practices, grounded in the notion that students who participate in the authentic work of science will access deeper levels of science understanding. The case study explored in this chapter turns the common integration of science in the service of ELA on its head, with the ML-PBL science curriculum informing student learning throughout the school day and providing a foundation for powerful integrated instruction. At a time when many teachers report that they have insufficient time to teach science, limited access to NGSS-aligned materials, and an inability to adjust the focus of their instruction, Ms. Hegg felt fortunate to have moved past each of these barriers as a result of her participation in the ML-PBL project.[20]

Ms. Hegg approached her first year enacting ML-PBL with the conviction that, with a strong and engaging science curriculum that promoted three-dimensional learning and integrated literacy and math, supported by rich PL experiences, she could redesign the rest of her day to support students in learning in all subjects. Moreover, she could certainly justify devoting a full hour to science every day. Ms. Hegg also chose to place special attention on two recommended literacy essentials by adding more interactive read-aloud experiences to the many shared readings and interactive read-alouds already included in the ML-PBL lessons; she also planned for systematic ongoing observation and assessment of the students' language and literacy development to formatively assess their progress toward learning goals and standards.[21]

In addition to providing opportunities for meeting all third-grade science standards, Ms. Hegg described her attempts to fully integrate science and literacy as allowing for greater opportunities for students' *literacy development* and for learning in all subjects. *Building common background knowledge* before and during units resulted in generating greater ownership of learning, increased interest and engagement, more questions for the Driving Question Board, and deeper comprehension of texts read. *Language development*—word usage, familiarity, and adding to vocabulary—strengthened student discourse and supported comprehension. *Discourse strategies* and repetitive *instructional routines* promoted deeper comprehension, sensemaking and figuring out—and Ms. Hegg found these to be valuable tools to use across all subject area instruction. *Developing thinking strategies* for reading informational texts, modeled by Ms. Hegg during read-alouds and shared reading, supported deeper comprehension and sensemaking.[22]

Finally, interest and engagement in learning more about science topics promoted *investigating the works of great authors* and *uncovering elements of their craft*; introducing reading for the purpose of story (literacy goals), then looking back when portions or illustrations provided support for (or additional examples of) what students were figuring out in science lessons, ensured seamless integration. Using ML-PBL, Ms. Hegg thus planned for her students to experience all of these rich opportunities for literacy development—and she did it in the context of science.

CHAPTER 9

Project-Based Learning Practices and Culturally Relevant Teaching

EMILY C. ADAH MILLER

The third-grade teacher, Luzmaria, is kneeling on the carpet, unfolding a large crinkled chart from the previous day's science lesson.[1] *She uses the day's Driving Question to start the lesson: "The question is, What do plants and animals need to survive?" The unveiling of the Driving Question always indicates that science has begun. The few students who have yet to join the circle move toward the carpet. Valeria, in a ballerina skirt, lightly twirls into a sitting position.*

Luzmaria's eyes sweep the semicircle; she glances briefly at each student and draws the children's focus. "Do you know what? I'd really like it if you all try to participate. Can you do it?" A few students—Fabian, Amanda, and Yasmin—answer with a drawn-out "yeah." Other students do not respond. Luzmaria glances at her lesson plan, face-up, next to her on the carpet. "We're going to make a chart." Amanda inches slightly forward. Luzmaria's voice is conversational in content and tone as she continues: "So you guys, you know we are talking about squirrels and what they need to survive. We talked about this issue. We went outside and looked at squirrels . . . a few times? Yes, that's true. But you see squirrels every day, right?" She looks up. "But what do they, the squirrels, have to have to survive?"

Luzmaria then repeats the Driving Question, as her finger traces the words. She is joined by a murmur of student voices. Luzmaria says, "Turn and talk with the person next to you. Tell them what you already know about this question." Luzmaria is following this lesson plan closely, exactly as written. It often appears that she has studied the lesson and aims for fidelity to the specifics in the lesson design. While teaching, she stops and reads parts of the plan verbatim and check her notes. However, this careful adherence to the lessons is abandoned by the end of the year, when Luzmaria understands the principles of PBL that undergird the design.

In this case, Luzmaria and her class change their relationship to project-based learning (PBL) over the course of the school year. As the principles of PBL gain importance in Luzmaria's understanding of how science is taught, she moves away from a strict observation of the PBL curriculum. Taking its place are adaptations to students' ideas and science practices to connect to community, culture, and context. The key ingredients of the PBL lessons remain, however: a Driving Question about science, student collaboration, open-ended discussions, and the development of authentic artifacts, which together underscore the underlying practice of responsiveness.[2] This case study tracks Luzmaria as she navigates the enactment of PBL materials and adapts the lessons to respond to the social and cultural practices of her students, the students' Latine heritage, and an unexpected science context.[3]

CONTEXT

Located west of the Great Lakes, in an urban, working-class neighborhood, Concord Elementary School is classified as a high-poverty school, with more than 80 percent of the students receiving free or reduced-price lunch. The eighteen students who make up this bilingual classroom identify as ethnically Hispanic, and all the students speak Spanish as their first language. Some of the students have recently arrived from other parts of the United States, or Latin America, and others are from first-generation immigrant families from Honduras and Mexico. The majority of the class lives in identical apartment buildings on the other side of a freeway that cuts through the neighborhood. They use an underground tunnel to walk to school.

Luzmaria has been teaching elementary school for five years. For several decades, she taught Spanish and Quechua as a limited-term employee at the local community college. She identifies as Mexican American and is a strong advocate for her students and their parents, some of whom struggle with finding work, housing, and other services. In an interview, Luzmaria described teaching science and bilingual education as deeply personal and political. She refers to the community readiness goals expected by the district, but adds, "I want (my students) to be proud of their heritage—it is their treasure. I tell them that all the time!" She explains how she sees heritage as connecting to science: "These guys, their interests and their goals, are part of who they are—of course. Who they are can't be separated from language, culture, heritage. Jimena wants to be a doctor. Why? Because she wants to help her mom!" Luzmaria describes teaching as a partnership between students and the teacher. She explains that she decided to learn PBL because it is more aligned with her approach to teaching than the program the district had adopted.

Engaging students' interest, positioning learning as relevant for the world, building on students' scientific experiences and culturally based knowledge, Luzmaria exemplifies the responsive teaching principles of PBL in her teaching. PBL is designed to motivate students through student-centered Driving Questions, use authentic artifacts to connect disciplinary learning with the local community, and create relevant contexts for students that hold sustained meaning for them socially and intellectually. Thus, it can be argued that PBL, at its core, aligns with culturally relevant pedagogy—an approach to teaching centered on high expectations, learning for social justice, and forming meaningful connections between what students are learning and their cultures, languages, and experiences.[4] When Luzmaria's adaptations move away from the curriculum as written, as in the instances shown in this case, PBL principles as intrinsically culturally responsive are adhered to, while at the same time the adaptations still provide opportunities for deep disciplinary learning.[5]

STUDENTS CREATE SCIENTIFIC PRACTICES BY BUILDING ON SOCIAL PRACTICES

There has been increasing attention on having students develop the disciplinary practice of constructing scientific explanations.[6] This involves students as early as kindergarten learning to support scientific claims with the use of appropriate evidence.[7] The Multiple Literacies in Project-Based Learning (ML-PBL) units are designed to develop the use of evidence as students engage with phenomena and scientific sensemaking. Throughout ML-PBL, teacher prompts help students wield evidence and listen for evidence in other's claims. These supportive features enable teachers to shift their practice; over time, they guide their students to seek evidence whenever they hear a claim and include evidence whenever they construct a claim. Other supportive features in the materials are the assignment of roles, such as "evidence checker," where the teacher assigns a student the job of checking for evidence; discourse structures such as "turn and talk" and "share out"; open-ended question prompts,; and discourse moves that support the teacher to go beyond asking "Who can repeat what was just said?" to questions that deepen student reasoning and clarify their ideas.

In the first week the Squirrels Unit—*Why do I see so many squirrels but can't find any stegosauruses?*—the students describe squirrels' needs and use their observations from field research to support the idea that squirrels meet all their needs outside. Luzmaria follows the lesson prompts exactly as written. She writes "evidence" on the whiteboard, defines it, and encourages the students to provide evidence in the discussion. When a student uses evidence in a claim, they are verbally rewarded: "Nice! I heard you use evidence!" Next, she presents an idea that is not in the lesson. She tells the class they will start listening for evidence all the time in science and when they hear it, they should all *whisper* the word "evidence." She explains that, through this stage whisper, they will receive immediate recognition for their effort. She asks the class, "Did anyone see outside that the squirrel needs water?" When there is no response, she prompts, "Look at your field notes." Josefina responds, "I do. He was in the bird water. He went in there!" Josefina shows her penciled note about the birdbath, where the students witnessed a squirrel drinking water. "Ah-ha!" Luzmaria exclaims, and addresses the class: "Did you hear it? Did Josefina use evidence?" Together, the students stage-whisper loudly in unison: "Evidence!" Josefina smiles.

The evidence whisper takes off in the class. What began as a Luzmaria's spontaneous idea evolves into a practice shared by the students, who continue to whisper "evidence" appropriately in many observed lessons throughout the year. Students eagerly raise their hands when asked to produce a claim; it seems they want to be responsible for causing the whispered acknowledgment. With almost conspiratorial looks and smiles among the students and their teacher, they delight in the dramatic and playful tone. The shared whisper is an added aural layer that changes the tenor of the science discussion. At the same time, it fosters science learning—highlighting a critical feature of the practice of constructing explanations.

FUNDS OF KNOWLEDGE AS EVIDENCE FOR SCIENTIFIC CLAIMS

Luzmaria was encouraged by the ML-PBL teacher-facing materials to honor students' Funds of Knowledge as a source of evidence. Funds of Knowledge are "historically accumulated and culturally developed bodies of knowledge and skills essential for household or individual functioning and well-being."[8] One of the ways Funds of Knowledge are supported in ML-PBL is through the inclusion of a short take-home interview in every unit that is based on the unit's Driving Question. This interview consists of the Driving Question and some follow-up questions and is designed to spark family dialogue and thus support students in making sense of the unit phenomena. The interview is translated—students are encouraged to use their first language for the interview. The home interview helps students consider experiences drawn from their familial, cultural, and linguistic community as valid and appropriate evidence for supporting scientific claims.[9]

In this first unit, "evidence" is defined as "what you have seen, or what others have seen, that backs up your claim." This definition is another prompt meant to encourage teachers to consider family stories as evidence. Luzmaria follows the prompts in the materials and encourages the students to ask each other for evidence when making claims. She does not differentiate evidence drawn from an experience (e.g., "One time, I saw the squirrel eating a pumpkin on the ground") from the more traditionally defined data collected in the classroom (e.g., "The squirrel book said that babies have no fur").

In the Toys Unit (*How can we design fun moving toys that any kid can build?*) the students continue to ask for evidence, but they begin to acknowledge the two different sources of evidence through the evidence whisper. When they anticipate classroom-based evidence, the exchange occurs without a whisper. They ask one another, "What's your evidence?" However, in other instances, the students also continue, unprompted, to use the evidence whisper as a request for, or shared acknowledgment of, a personal, cultural, or community-based science story. When some classmates, especially those who tell stories in science, begin to support a scientific claim, the students use the evidence whisper. It is as if to say, "This is the kind of evidence we love to hear—please go on!"

The curriculum supports a more traditional use of evidence—the objective data that support a claim or an argument—as well as the stories about science experiences; however, in this class, stories carry the extra excitement of the dramatic stage whisper. This highlighting of students' cultural knowledge and use of family experiences as classroom-based evidence is especially pronounced in the third and fourth units.

UNDERSTANDING EVIDENCE AS SCIENTIFIC AND SOCIAL PRACTICE

In the Birds Unit (*How can I help the birds near my school grow up and thrive?*)—the students read a fictional text about a migrant community in the Middle East: *Four Feet, Two Sandals*.[10] The students are prompted to consider the reasons people migrate and compare these with bird migration. Luzmaria follows the lesson, inviting the students to share stories of their own migration to the United States. She gathers three student ideas about the migration of people to serve as evidence for claims about birds and people, as written in the curriculum, but the students resist: they want to hear more of their own migration stories. Luzmaria points at the Driving Question Board and starts the discussion:

LUZMARIA: Let's go back to the Driving Question: *Do people migrate for the same reason as birds?*

JORDAN: From Venezuela to here? Yes, I know someone.

LUZMARIA: Jordan, can you tell me about them? Um, explicame de algún Venezolano alguien que emigró [Tell me about a Venezuelan who emigrated].

ALEJANDRO: Yes, I know [someone]!

LUZMARIA: Why did they move?

ALEJANDRO: Because—

STUDENTS [IN A WHISPER]: "Evidence!"

ALEJANDRO: —they didn't want to be there anymore. They were tired about the style of living there. They want a new beginning.

In this last part of the dialogue, Alejandro changes his voice to mimic someone he heard. Luzmaria then invites the class to contribute their thoughts:

LUZMARIA: Can you—anyone—help us out here? Tell me about why they moved?

JORDAN: My cousin and mom and dad . . . moved because the situation in their country was terrible.

LUZMARIA: Like in what way?

JORDAN: Like not having money to eat and having to bargain.

VALERIA: And I know someone. Many people.

STUDENTS [IN A WHISPER]: Evidence!

VALERIA: The troubles they have with the president all that. It's like, problems. Like, it's hard to explain, the price of the things are—growing and growing.

LUZMARIA: We know how birds migrate. Do you think that birds move for the same reasons that people do?

VALERIA: I think that in certain ways they do. Because of the food and the place. But I think it's kind of alike.

Luzmaria explains why the use of evidence from student's lives was particularly important in the migration lesson and discussed the growing social practice: "It's funny, all the kids wanted to talk about something. They wanted to go around the circle [because] we were talking about the migration and they really, really like to share. Azul, she is opening up. It takes a long time for her to open up and want to share." Luzmaria's students are figuring out a meaningful problem—*How can I help birds near the school grow up and thrive?*—and are constructing their own life experiences to do so. At the same time, by hearing each other's stories, they are engaging in practices important to science learning.

Luzmaria suspects that the storytelling cue that the students created was part of their Latine heritage. She says, "I think using stories is cultural for some of the students. You know how animated Hugo gets when he tells a story? He moves around the room and moves his arms, takes on roles? I saw his dad do that!" Asking for evidence was an opportunity to prop up underrepresented resources and infuse them into science sensemaking. The culturally relevant teaching demonstrated by Luzmaria in this case is aligned with the PBL approach because of its emphasis on authentic contexts that are meaningful to students, which in this case are drawn from cultural and community-based knowledge.[11] The acceptance of the nontraditional application of evidence as both an epistemic and social lever is aligned with the deeply rooted responsive approach of PBL.

PBL is student-centered, and all the practices are derived, in part, in response to the unique combinations of knowledge contained in the group. PBL practices foster motivation, individuality, and creativity in the service of disciplinary learning.[12] In this example, we see students not only developing a sophisticated understanding of evidence, but also making important connections with scientific ideas. The students are considering the needs of organisms and developing an understanding that behaviors of animals relate to their needs for survival. In the unit, Luzmaria's students initially think that birds migrate because they are cold, so they struggle to figure out why some birds migrate and others overwinter. However, by helping students bring forth their own experiences, and the experiences of their families, they make the connection between the availability of resources and animals relocating to a new area, which is one of the performance expectations in the NGSS.

ARTIFACTS CONNECT TO THE DRIVING QUESTION AND BUILD ON STUDENTS' LATINE HERITAGE

A feature of PBL is the development of an artifact that represents the aggregation of student learning over time. The commensurate PBL practice involves developing an artifact that is authentic to the community.[13] In ML-PBL, teachers are encouraged to position the artifact as a central focus in their lessons and as an ongoing response to the Driving Question. The next example describes this PBL practice, showing how Luzmaria adapts the artifact written in the unit. In doing so, she creates a culturally relevant additional artifact centered on a Latin American connection.

In unit 3, the students complete fieldwork to identify native birds that live near their school. They then conduct a resource inventory of the nearby environment and collect data about available food sources; they figure out that some resources are readily available and others are scarce. Next, the students use phenology (the study of seasons) to explain which birds migrate and why. They choose a bird to research and gather information about its foraging behaviors and its life cycle and to determine how to help it. For the final artifact, they design and place a bird feeder near their school. They present the feeder to their community and explain how it could help birds grow up and thrive. All of these activities are enacted by Luzmaria's class, as designed by the ML-PBL program.

The unit was designed to solicit students' connections to culture, family, and language. Again, as described earlier, Luzmaria asks the students to interview a family member about a bird story; they then write about these stories in English language arts. During science class, the students share photos about birds of Latin America and write down the national birds of some of the students' home countries.

In the third week of the unit, they add an artifact that is meaningful and authentic to the local community. During the week, a mother asks Luzmaria if she and her daughter can describe a bird issue that is "near to her heart." Luzmaria agrees, and the Spanish-speaking parent gives a presentation to the class with her daughter, Valeria. Together, they talk about how they want to stop the *Semana Santa* custom of selling brightly dyed chicks in the *feria*, or outdoor market. Valeria and her mother explain how harmful the custom is for the chicks' development, as the dyes create respiratory problems for the chicks, along with cognitive issues. Sitting next to her mother, Valeria joins her in helping the others understand the importance of the issue.

In this instance, Valeria has initiated an immediate, urgent redesign of the unit's artifact. It is mid-March and almost *Semana Santa*, which means the dyeing and selling of chicks is imminent. Luzmaria's students are moved to action. They decide they need to do some research and then educate others in their school about the issue. They read websites, watch online informational articles, and then put together a PowerPoint in Spanish, advocating for the end of this practice. They make a presentation to the fourth- and fifth-grade bilingual classes, write emails persuading their relatives not to buy the chicks, and many of them collaborate on a piece in the school newsletter about the harmfulness of the practice. Through these activities, the students connect science with their families and the local Latin American community.[14]

VALERIA: Do you see how these chicks are colored? What do you think of this?
ANTHONY: I think it's quite pretty.
VALERIA: You think it's pretty? But what do you think it does to the little chick? Do you think it's good for it?
ADRIAN: No, it's not good for it.
FERNANDA: And why is that?
LISET: Well, I don't know. I know that it's not good for it because they put that dye on them.
EFRAIM: But it's pretty?
ALAN: Yes, they look pretty, but I don't know if it's good.
VALERIA: And what do you think it does to the chick?
ALEJANDRO: I'm not sure but I will say that it's bad for them, for some reason.
LUZMARIA [LAUGHING]: You are also dyed.
ANTHONY: Yeah my hair is dyed green.
VALERIA: How can we help them? If the dye makes them sick?

LISET: I don't know! I would take the dye off them, take them to the veterinarian.
STUDENT: How would you take off the dye?
ADRIAN: With a little bath? My mom would know what to do.[15]

In this example, the adapted artifact draws on cultural and linguistic strengths, which defines culturally relevant teaching.[16] The *Semana Santa* artifact captures the students' attention and sustains their learning. Some students study chicks at home on computers, and some ask to work on the PowerPoint and the newsletter during lunch. The students also build a bird feeder: the unit's engineering performance expectations require that an object be designed, iterated, and improved according to certain criteria, which would not have been met by the *Semana Santa* social action. Thus, the final artifact designed in the written materials is enriched but not abandoned, and Luzmaria has still addressed the learning goals.

Luzmaria's and her students' response of reshaping the artifact from a bird feeder to include a solution to a humanitarian problem embeds cultural resources with rigorous disciplinary learning goals. Helping the chicks survive is an experience that stems from the unit's Driving Question and lesson-level ideas concerning adaptation and survival. The students are making sense of, and applying, the science idea that there are critical and specific points in an animal's life cycle. The curriculum enactment thus maintains coherence and meets the learning goals—and, with the additional artifact, connects with families.

Moreover, Luzmaria adapts the written design by following the interests of the students: a principle embedded in the features of PBL. This enactment allows for culturally relevant pedagogy through the incorporation of culturally based experience and knowledge. Here, she is reaching out, bringing the families in on the topic but with a culturally relevant and meaningful activity. As part of enacting the PBL feature of an artifact—the PBL practice of connecting the artifact in an authentic way with the community-based problem—Luzmaria is responsive to her students.

DRIVING QUESTION AS DRIVEN BY AN UNPREDICTED SCIENCE CONTEXT

The final third-grade ML-PBL unit is Plants. This unit is designed toward the development of an authentic artifact that connects with the community.[17] The Driving Question for the Plants Unit—*How can we plan gardens in our com-*

munity to grow plants for food?—is answered through the design of a garden plot that may mitigate the effects of hazardous weather, such as flooding. The focus of the unit is on the life cycle of plants, the difference between climate and weather, and how engineers design for hazardous weather to protect communities.

Luzmaria and her class begin to grow food in their classroom's small designated garden plot. The students enthusiastically press the seeds a few inches down in measured rows. They engage with texts about how chocolate grows in a very different climate, and they create precipitation graphs to contrast that climate with their own. However, the class veers away from the curriculum to make the artifact relevant. Aligned with the PBL principles, Luzmaria again responds to context and student interest and focuses on an urgent problem: the students' need to find a solution for the beetles that are eating their plants:. "They learned a lot right away: How things grow and don't grow. They see all the dead stuff too. Why the whole plot of basil was attacked by beetles and blight? What happens when plants don't make it? Blight. It was a Japanese beetles' orgy!"

Luzmaria requests ideas from the students, who in turn ask their family members what they might do about the insects. She asks the class, "I know a lot of you want to share. Anthony, what do you want to say?" Anthony replies, "Can I say in Spanish?"[18]

LUZMARIA: Mmmm. That's okay. But look, some bugs, some tiny bugs, come to your plant to eat it and you have to get rid of them. How would you do it?

ANTHONY: I could . . . I could put some poison on them that doesn't kill the plant.

LUZMARIA: Like what type of poison do you mean?

ANTHONY: One that scares them away. Just that.

LUZMARIA: One that scares away the bugs, but doesn't do anything to the plant. Could you give me an example?

ADRIAN: My uncle told me that I could also put caps filled with beer on the potting soil. This I think would make the bugs leave it alone.

FERNANDO: Silly idea, that cannot work! Plants need sun and water.

Luzmaria gathers the students' ideas, and they decide to research the solution on the internet. She shares, "We were battling them all summer; I hated to kill them. You would kill a bunch on the tree, thousands of them! The beetles would fall into this bag. It was water with detergent in it. The kids could pick them off with their hand and then whip them in the water. It was really gross but—it's food!"

Here, the context for learning is reinforcing an authentic divergence from curriculum materials but remains coherent with the unit's Driving Question, and consistent with PBL practices. The class is adhering to aspects of the unit design, as it is centered on learning about plant growth and on engineering a problem-solving design. The students are also able to address the unit's standards. The materials and their framing of the authenticity of PBL emphasize student interest in real, not contrived, problems that resonate with the community. Through immersion in an authentic problem, the students are developing scientific and engineering practices, such as iterating solutions based on constraints and criteria, investigation, modeling solutions, and defining the problem. They are also using the authentic problem to revisit some of the environmental ideas of predator and prey.

In the enactment of the final unit, we see Luzmaria veering from the written design by responding to an unexpected science context and adapting the problem the students are working on. Here, she is striving to create relevance and meaningfulness to the students in a manner that is complementary to the PBL. Instead of studying weather, climate, and engineering for hazardous weather events, the students develop knowledge about plants, and how plants change during their life cycle, to solve the problem of an insect attack on their vegetables. The phenomenon remains, as do the lesson-level questions, but the unit problem and the unit solution become adapted to the context.

CONCLUSION

This case study shows how adaptations from the materials as they were originally designed were consistent with PBL practices because they promoted authentic connection to the Driving Question, student interest, social practices, and figuring out meaningful solutions to problems. In this case, the principles of PBL meant an engagement and inclusion of underrepresented perspectives. The three examples from Luzmaria's classroom demonstrate that, in a community, responsiveness is integral to PBL and underlies the features so strongly that teachers can adapt their units as needed.

In the first example, the socially and culturally based use of evidence complemented the students' use of the objective, and more traditional, scientifically sanctioned use of evidence. In the second, students' experiences and knowledge were essentially brought into the canon. Students became responsible for learning about each other's cultures and experiences and they learned to leverage the experiences for shared knowledge construction. In the final example, the classroom community developed expanded definitions and meanings of science to address the problem in the garden and sought out lived experiences and culturally based intellectual resources.

In these examples, we see how PBL's focus on leveraging students' social and cultural strengths through collaboration and discussion promotes inclusion and also promotes teachers' developing responsive practices. Through highlighting social practices and culturally based intellectual resources as a means to learn more, PBL practices are part of connecting the ideas that students bring to school to make the learning relevant. The adaptations Luzmaria made to the units reflected the PBL practices and showed that they are commensurate with culturally relevant pedagogy. Embracing PBL in her adaptations while adhering to the intent of the materials, Luzmaria also met the learning goals—thus successfully using PBL practices to enhance student engagement in the service of enabling deep disciplinary learning of science ideas.

CHAPTER 10

Growing into Leadership Through Project-Based Learning

DEBORAH PEEK-BROWN

In Ms. Butler's science class, learning is a community affair for students and the teacher. She says that she feels more like a conductor of a symphony than the holder of knowledge. "I have been letting them bring their own information to science and then weaving it together to make it something that everybody can take part in." Her interest in making learning something that everyone can take part in goes beyond her own classroom. After nine months of participating in the Multiple Literacies in Project-Based Learning (ML-PBL) project, she has become a lead teacher supporting change in teaching strategies across her large urban district. Through her experiences as an ML-PBL teacher, Ms. Butler has mobilized change in her school and district by sharing practices with colleagues, collaboratively developing and sharing resource materials, and leading professional learning (PL). Her history has made it possible for her to take leadership in her own knowledge-building and leadership across her school district.

The transformation from novice ML-PBL teacher to facilitator of PL did not occur in a vacuum. Ms. Butler's capacity to act purposefully and constructively to direct her own professional growth and her desire to contribute to the growth of her colleagues is the very definition of teacher agency.[1] The intersection between her aspirations as a teacher and her experiences in ML-PBL provides insight into the factors that influenced her journey. This case describes how Ms. Butler became involved in ML-PBL, her experiences enacting the curriculum and participating in PL, and how she extended those experiences to influence other teachers in her district.

THE BEGINNING OF THE JOURNEY

Ms. Butler has been working in a large urban district with 90 percent low-income African American students for over twenty-five years and still expresses a passion for teaching: "Well, it's kind of like my calling. I've always kind of known it, even when I didn't want to admit it to myself. I knew I was going to be a teacher, and I've been teaching ever since, you know, even playing school as a child." Ms. Butler has always had a passion for science. Although her degree is in elementary education, she majored in science and English and she has taught only science for over two decades. Currently she teaches science to a different third-, fourth-, or fifth-grade class every forty minutes at a K–5 elementary school. From the configuration of the room to the decorations on the walls, her students are confronted with science experiences as soon as they walk through the door.

Ms. Butler's state adopted the Next Generation Science Standards (NGSS). Prior to that, the state standards included content-based rather than performance-based learning goals. Although there were inquiry-based learning goals, these were separate from the content standards and resulted in teaching content and inquiry goals separately. Ms. Butler's ideas around science instruction reflected this focus on content. Even with this statewide focus, she remembers feeling that teaching content without firsthand experiences was inadequate:

> I used the [district-provided text] chapter vocabulary . . . I would hook in the investigations to help them understand vocabulary. So when we're talking about Newton's laws of motion, I would do investigations that would show Newton's laws of motion to reinforce or introduce the words related to the content. Whatever the vocabulary was, that's what the topic of the investigations became.

The vision of the NGSS calls for shifting students from learning isolated facts to figuring out phenomena. Many efforts helped teachers make this shift in their instruction. Workshops were conducted to support teachers in moving their instruction from passively "learning about science" to actively "figuring out" why events occur. Although Ms. Butler's district leaders informed teachers of the coming changes, limited opportunities for PL about the NGSS existed within the district. Because of this lack of opportunities, she joined her county's science meetings to obtain more information and prepare herself for the shift: "I first started hearing about the NGS three or four years before it was adopted and I thought, 'This is what's coming. It's going to change everything,' and I wanted to find out more information."

The intermediate school district held monthly meetings for all science teachers. These meetings consisted of guest speakers from different school districts, the state science department, and publishers describing new teaching strategies and curriculum materials. Since the NGSS was new, the resources focused on creating a more student-centered classroom. Ms. Butler enthusiastically embraced this change and implemented many of the strategies introduced: "I started changing my teaching at that point and I started moving away from vocabulary and added more projects. I started trying to do centers and have each group doing a hands-on activity that would really be related to whatever the topic was in hopes that the kids would kind of start being less dependent on me and have the kids doing more of the work."

Although Ms. Butler tried many different science programs, none of them seemed to completely meet the needs of her students as she shifted her instruction to align with the NGSS. The science programs that she tried were more student-centered than her previous instruction but still focused on students reading about science. She continued to seek new opportunities to develop a classroom environment that centered around students experiencing science. After reading about ML-PBL as a learning system that included a full year of curriculum materials as well as the development of a PL community around the implementation of the NGSS, Ms. Butler decided that this was the opportunity she had been looking for. She explains, "I had gone through everything that the county had to offer, and the district wasn't offering anything as of yet. And so I saw ML-PBL, and I thought this would help me to be ready to teach the new standards."

JOINING THE ML-PBL TEAM

In the fall of 2017, a new district science director, Ms. Fox, was hired. Ms. Fox was very interested in expanding opportunities for teachers to learn about the shift in instruction necessary for teachers to embrace the NGSS. She explains the challenge for her teachers this way:

> The past couple of years, we've been transitioning to teaching and learning in the science classroom with the adoption of the new science standards, also known as NGSS. We're moving from just learning about science to figuring out phenomena, which is a very different way of teaching and learning than we have experienced in school, and it is a big transition for teachers and for students. We know that the new concepts and tools used in the ML-PBL units help support

children in the knowledge and skills they need to be successful in all of their classes and more importantly in their lives.

Ms. Fox not only supported her district's participation in the ML-PBL, but she also initiated a partnership between the university and the district to support increased PL for all science teachers, K–12. She actively recruited and recommended schools to participate in ML-PBL. As district science director, Ms. Fox exemplifies what scholars describe as best practices in leaders who recognize and support the development of their staff in gaining ownership and experience in learning about new instructional opportunities. Her willingness to extend her knowledge and develop opportunities for others to do the same represents a key feature of distributed leadership.[2] .

Ms. Fox's leadership gave space for the experiences that led to Ms. Butler's professional growth. Through Ms. Fox's recruitment efforts, Ms. Butler learned about the project: "Yes, I signed up for doing ML-PBL on the district website. I saw the study for third grade and I'm like, 'I'm not sure what this is.' I had no idea what I was getting involved with at first. I thought it was something that could help me. I had no idea where it would lead me. I was not sure where I was going but I knew I wasn't satisfied where I was at."

Given her interest and experience, Ms. Butler was invited to participate in the ML-PBL project. The ML-PBL Summer Institute included three full days of developing a teacher learning community around the features of project-based learning (PBL) within the context of the first ML-PBL unit. During the year, three full-day sessions were planned—one for each of the three units. The sessions were led by a collaborative team of university researchers and experienced ML-PBL teachers who had participated in the development of the units.

One of the main goals of these sessions was to provide opportunities for teachers to experience the lessons firsthand and then reflect on the features of PBL they experienced. Teachers collaboratively participated in scientific practices such as making observations, analyzing data, and drawing models. They experienced the use of discourse as a responsive teaching practice that equitably supports students in developing a shared understanding of natural phenomena. Through these experiences and discussions, they identified the big science ideas that were investigated and the teaching practices used to promote equitable sensemaking.

During PL, Ms. Butler experienced the first ML-PBL unit, *Why do I see so many squirrels but can't find any stegosauruses?* Teachers were presented with multiple opportunities to experience phenomena by participating in lessons in the same way that their students would, but as adult learners. The three-day summer sessions allowed them to enact key lessons, such as going on a walk outside to observe squirrels, investigating squirrel skulls to identify structural adaptations, and developing models to explain squirrel survival. Teachers also observed examples of student experiences through videos of teachers in ML-PBL classrooms using strategies that supported student discourse and social-emotional learning goals. Small-group discussions allowed teachers to reflect on how the strategies they experienced could be implemented in their classrooms. Ms. Butler saw great value in these PL sessions:

> I really like the way the PDs [professional development sessions] gave you some foreshadowing of what's to come and what to expect. That made it so much easier when I did it in my own class because I kind of went through it as the students would have. But doing it as a teacher at the same time made it a lot easier when I started doing it with my students. I'm like, "Okay, I know from their point of view this is what they were thinking because this is what I was thinking." As a teacher, I know how to get them past that into where I need them to be. Just from being exposed to it in the PD was so helpful. I started going to the meetings and going through and finding out all about it, and I really enjoyed the difference that it could make in the students and in me as well.

Experiencing the features unique to ML-PBL through collaborative activities, discussions, and the development of artifacts created an authentic learning community among the teachers that continued throughout the school year.

EXPERIENCES WITH ML-PBL

After experiencing the summer PL sessions, however, Ms. Butler was not yet fully convinced of the effectiveness of PBL. She was concerned that the instructional time needed for the units (six to eight weeks) would make it difficult to keep her students engaged. In the fall of 2018, she began enacting the ML-PBL curriculum. After seeing her students' reactions to the unit, she made a shift in her thinking:

> Going through the PDs and introducing the Squirrel[s] Unit, I was thinking kids are not going to want to learn about squirrels for as long as this unit is. You

> know, 'cause I've never stayed on a unit that long. I was very surprised that the kids not only wanted to but they were like, "Okay, we can't do this anymore?" We were about to switch and do the Toys Unit. They still wanted to do more with squirrels, and that surprised me. Their reactions to it were really good, and that's pretty much what kind of hooked me.

Ms. Butler described her skepticism about this shift. The issue of pacing is a major challenge for many teachers trying to shift their teaching to an extended investigation of phenomena that allows students time to "figure things out." Initially, teachers did not see the multiple opportunities afforded to students to use big ideas and scientific practices during the course of a unit or even the entire year. This created a tension between the desire to linger on parts of the curriculum that students find highly engaging or challenging and the need to move on to complete the unit. Ms. Butler was faced with this challenge, as she only saw her students two or three days a week. While this new pacing was difficult, after trying lessons with her students and seeing their reaction, she became convinced of the benefits. Many other features of PBL were new to Ms. Butler; however, she found some features such as the use of the Driving Question and modeling immediately valuable.

SUPPORTING FEATURES OF PROJECT-BASED LEARNING—THE DRIVING QUESTION

During her first summer PL sessions, Ms. Butler worked through the process of observing phenomena and generating her own questions through the lens of the unit's Driving Question, *Why do I see so many squirrels but can't find any stegosauruses?* As Ms. Butler experienced key lessons in the unit, the ML-PBL facilitator continually referred back to the participants' questions and encouraged them to ask and post new questions on the Driving Question Board (see figure 10.1).[3] Teachers were asked what questions had been answered and how these answers were related to the Driving Question. Ms. Butler began to see the Driving Question as a tool to give students ownership, purpose, and connection throughout the unit.

Two months after starting the unit, Ms. Butler was still referencing the Driving Question to help students make connections between ideas they investigated.

FIGURE 10.1 Sample Driving Question Board

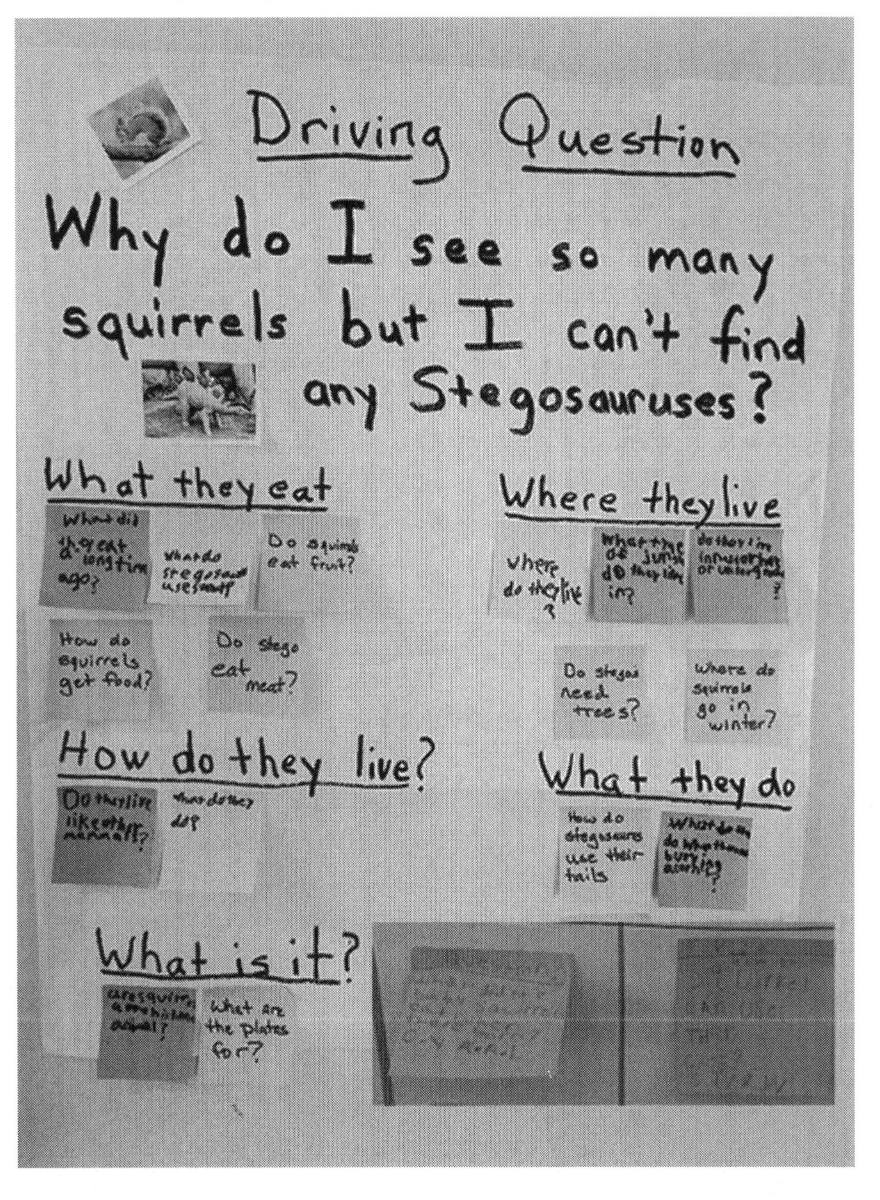

MS. BUTLER: How is the squirrel's structure unique and important?

TYLER: Their legs. His nails. He can climb up trees and run. His legs are small.

MS. BUTLER: Why do some animals like the stegosaurus die out, and some animals live?

TYLER: 'Cuz they can't—when things change like the temperature, they can't survive because they don't have the right structures.

MS. BUTLER: What other organisms live in the squirrels' environment, and does the squirrel need [them] to survive? Remember we worked on this one before.

Here, Ms. Butler pulled out a chart/model of the squirrel habitat and shows it to the students. Students continued to discuss information from past lessons that they could use as evidence to support their ideas and to answer the unit's Driving Question about what happened to the stegosaurus.

Although the concept of the Driving Question was new to Ms. Butler, she willingly used it it to support students in explaining phenomena and connecting artifacts to relevant learning experiences. Even though she was initially skeptical of students sustaining engagement in these phenomena over an extended period of time, she found that features of ML-PBL, like the Driving Question, kept her students interested and excited about studying squirrels.

During this first unit, Ms. Butler used a great deal of scaffolded questioning because she did not feel that her students understood how to ask their own questions. She found support for assisting her students in this area during the PL sessions she attended for the second ML-PBL unit: *How can we design fun moving toys that any kid can build?"* At the beginning of the session, when teachers were encouraged to share their successes and challenges, Ms. Butler found that she was not the only teacher whose students struggled with asking questions. She was pleased to learn a new strategy for supporting students in generating questions introduced in this session. Teachers shot off toy rockets and then used their observations to develop questions. Ms. Butler found that this strategy, coupled with experiences in the previous unit, created a big improvement in her students' asking questions:

> The biggest differences were the use of the Driving Question Board in Squirrels compared to Toys. In the Squirrel[s] Unit, it was like pulling teeth. The kids were looking at me as if I was speaking a different language. They didn't understand what it meant to ask questions. They couldn't get it. By the time we got to the Toys Unit, they seemed like they had been doing it for years and they knew

> exactly what to do. By the time we got to Toys, mostly everybody was able to ask their own question, and the ones who couldn't knew that they could talk with a partner and come up with a question.

Through use of the Driving Question and the associated activities, Ms. Butler was beginning to see a transformation in her students as well as in herself: "In particular, I would have to say, for example, the practice of coming up with the questions, asking questions that lead to more questions, so that they can find the answer. When we first started asking questions about the bottle rocket, how it was moving, and coming up with ways to describe what they were actually seeing—in my mind, that's them becoming the scientist."

Ms. Butler's openness to trying new strategies gave her an opportunity to change the culture of her classroom such that students were taking ownership by asking and answering their own questions. She saw that she was no longer leading every discussion. This change only motivated her to do more.

SUPPORTING THE USE OF SCIENTIFIC PRACTICES—DEVELOPING MODELS

Motivated by her strong desire to improve the learning environment for her students, Ms. Butler embraced scientific practices that were unfamiliar to her. Developing models was a scientific practice that was very new for both Ms. Butler and her students. Although it was challenging, she pressed forward using the strategies she obtained through the PL sessions: "In the beginning, they struggled because they just didn't have enough background information, but after we started moving into it and doing it more and coming up with the models and all the things that they need to include in the model, the struggle became less."

The strategy of supporting student modeling through developing collaborative class models was also introduced in the Saturday PL session for the Toys Unit. During this session, the facilitators developed collaborative models with the teachers to explain the motion of a toy rocket. After experiencing the lesson, teachers reflected on how the facilitator used the teachers' ideas in developing the model rather than prescribing common conventions ahead of time. This strategy of preferencing student ideas can be seen as Ms. Butler describes supporting her students in developing a class model:

> I created a model as they were creating a model. We were doing it together. It's like, "Okay. How are we going to show speed?" They came up with some ideas and, "Okay. This is what we agree on. We're going to use three lines if it's going

really fast, two lines for medium, one line for slow. How are we going to show what direction it's going to go in?" They said, "Arrows." "Well, how are we going to show how strong the force is?" "Well, we're making the arrows bigger and wider." So we did it as a class and we made some classroom models. Now I don't have to make the model with them. I can just have them list what's going to be needed in the model and they're on their own.

Through her experiences in PL sessions, Ms. Butler was not only able to develop her students' use of modeling, she also understood the value in the practice:

I think developing models provides students with the fact that there's not only one way to get to your answer to the question. You can draw a model. You can write it out. If you don't like drawing, you can write about it and just do a little bit of drawing. You can do a lot of drawing with a little bit of writing. You can explain it to somebody else as part of your group and your ideas get put into somebody else's model. Those kids who are just totally oral and can just speak it, they can still get their ideas on paper just by having someone else write it out. I think it definitely gives kids more opportunity to show what they know in many different ways.

Most of Ms. Butler's classes were groups of very diverse learners with reading levels above and below grade level by as much as two years. Ms. Butler felt that modeling truly supported equitable sensemaking in her class. It gave all of her students the opportunity to figure out phenomena. High achievers were not stifled, and struggling students were not discouraged. Everyone was able to engage in the scientific process at their own level:

I have one kid in mind, the one kid with a very busy model. He's definitely a high achiever. He's the one who knew about static electricity, and positive and negative, and attract and repel. He knew about all of that before we even started the unit, and he created a model to show his group members what he was talking about. I had him put it on the board. So he is pretty much a high achiever—and still, even with him knowing all that information, he was still able to connect it to the new information about the non-contact forces, balanced and unbalanced forces. So I think it does help them as well.

Later in the interview, Ms. Butler continued:

I think, for struggling students, modeling seemed like it took a little bit of the stress off because there wasn't a whole lot of writing. I told them that they can draw the pictures as opposed to just writing about it. So once I took the pressure off of writing, they started writing to the best of their ability. I said, "Well, you have to give me at least one sentence describing what it is that you have drawn so that way someone else will know what it is." Once I took some of the pressure off, they started writing a whole lot more than what they would have if I had said, "Okay. Give me three sentences."

Ms. Butler found that sharing ideas and thinking was just as important for teacher learning as it was for students. She found that PL not only gave her an opportunity to learn from the facilitators, but she was also able to share and learn from other teachers:

> I do get ideas from other teachers who were doing the same unit. Sometimes—I don't know—hit a brick wall and don't know how to get through. Then during the PL session, another teacher would tell me what they did to make it easier for the kids. It was during the end of the Toy[s] Unit, and I was just talking about how to pull the unit all together and wrap it up. In the beginning of the unit, the students did interviews with kindergartners about toys, but I never thought about it again. That's an interview, that lesson is done, put a check in the box. She said her students went back to the kindergarten and the kids got a chance to explain the changes that they made to the toys and why they made them.

Ms. Butler continued to have many opportunities to share with her colleagues as she participated in a full-day PL session and a short virtual afterschool session for each unit. In the informal virtual sessions, Ms. Butler began sharing more and more with other teachers. She found that when other teachers shared problems, she often had solutions. Her experiences with the students were helpful to others and their experiences were helpful to her. The value that Ms. Butler found in collaborating with her peers and her enthusiasm for creating new learning environments for her students played a significant role in her ML-PBL journey.

BECOMING A TEACHER LEADER

Ms. Butler's role as a teacher leader began informally, as sharing with other teachers became a normal practice for her during the ML-PBL professional learning sessions. Later in the same year that she was participating in the ML-PBL project for the third grade, her district was also piloting other ML-PBL units for the fourth grade. Because she taught science to multiple grades, Ms. Butler attended those PL sessions as well:

> When I went to the district PL sessions for fourth grade, it was kind of introducing everything to the majority of the teachers. That's where I found out that I

> had a lot of information that other teachers didn't have and I became one of the experts in the room. During the PL session, we were talking, and it would be in a small group. I would let them know where I was in the unit and what I was doing. At first I'd be talking to one or two people, and I looked up and I had the attention of the whole group because they were all listening at this point.

Ms. Butler found that her expertise was not only being noticed by science teachers. As the designated science teacher for her elementary school, other teachers would bring their classes to her for science once a week. The teacher would sit in class with their students, as they were responsible for teaching science to the students at other times during the week. Even though these teachers were not a part of the ML-PBL project, they noticed something different about the class discussions during science:

> Twice a day, teachers came in my room with their class and they were supposed to stay with their kids. They watched me use the talk moves and how I gave the talk move cards to the kids to use as well.[4] The teachers were just floored when they started seeing the kids interact with each other and they heard their responses in the conversation. They saw that it was orderly and calm, and the kids were actually listening to each other. One teacher said that she wished she could have discussions like this and asked if she could borrow the talk move cards. The next time I went to a PD, I asked if I could get some cards to give to my colleagues.

Without realizing it, Ms. Butler was stepping into the role of teacher leader as she began to use the strategies she gained in the ML-PBL project to support the professional growth of other teachers. Others in the district science department were taking notice too. The elementary science coordinator noticed these changes during district-led PL sessions for fourth grade:

> Ms. Butler is a very quiet person. I wasn't even aware that she was an ML-PBL teacher until she started to open up and share her classroom experiences with the group. She was always so excited to talk about how she used the ML-PBL strategies and made them work for her and her students. I recognized that she would make a great teacher leader because of her knowledge about the units and willingness to help. Every time I would pose a question to the group, asking if anyone tried a specific strategy or had any feedback, even questions, about a component of an activity or lesson, she was always willing to share how it worked for her and her students.

MS. BUTLER TODAY

The science department in Ms. Butler's district became very interested in using ML-PBL at each grade level due to the positive experiences of third-grade teachers in the study. As the district began plans to expand the use of ML-PBL science units to more teachers, there was a need for more teacher support. The elementary science coordinator in collaboration with the ML-PBL researchers began to identify teacher leaders who could lead PL sessions for each grade level. Many of the teacher leaders identified were a part of the original curriculum development study and had been teaching the units for two to three years. They also participated in some of the subsequent PL sessions that were part of the study as panelists sharing their ML-PBL experiences with first-year teachers. The changes observed in Ms. Butler made her a great candidate to take on this role. She was the only teacher asked to become a teacher leader with less than one year of experience teaching the units. Ms. Butler saw this new challenge as another opportunity to grow professionally and help other teachers to grow as well.

> I was going to district PDs for fourth and fifth grade when the elementary science coordinator asked if I would like to be one of the teacher leaders and do professional learning sessions with her. That is when I realized that I do have something that others might want to know. Before being asked to be a teacher leader I thought, you know, "I'm doing this [ML-PBL]; it's in my classroom and that's as far as it goes." I realized that I do have information that others may want to hear and could learn from. I thought, "Why not? I can try it and see. If I don't like it, I can always stop." Even though it put me outside of my comfort zone, I wanted to stretch and do something more.

Lack of experience notwithstanding, Ms. Butler was adept at taking her own experiences and translating them into the identified needs of her peers. She was so aware of her own struggles that she could easily relate to other teachers and help develop solutions that were authentic to their classroom experiences implementing PBL. The elementary science coordinator for the district recognized these traits right away as Ms. Butler began working with other teachers in the district:

> Ms. Butler always had great ideas for tweaking little things to make them fit the situation; like before the district was able to provide teachers with talk move cards, she suggested to the group that they make copies and create signs for

> each table or group so that the students could easily refer to them during group discussions. I believe that she even printed her group roles and responsibilities on the back. She worked amazingly well with other teachers. She understood the struggles that our teachers face on a daily basis because she was right there with them! And she always helped other teachers see the positive in the situation and helped them figure out how we can make it better, rather than dwell on what cannot be changed.

These were great contributions to the district PL sessions; however, Ms. Butler was not satisfied with just tangentially supporting teachers. She wanted to be able to lead. She continued to push herself to learn and do more:

> I know I'm not where the other teacher leaders are because they have more experience in doing this than I do. I think right now that my niche is that I bring authentic reactions to what students are doing and what teachers are going through. I'm just like a few steps ahead of where they are so I can still remember it being really new and my feelings about it. I think it helps the teachers who are new at this. I think that eventually I'll be—you know, if I keep stretching and doing more—I will be at a spot where I'll be more at ease in taking on more of the instructional part of the professional learning sessions.

Ms. Butler's desire to stretch beyond her comfort level in order to direct her own professional growth along with the preparation and skills she gained through participation in the ML-PBL project put her in the perfect position to move from ML-PBL teacher to teacher leader. Even as she was taking on this new role of supporting PL, she continued to teach the units to her own students and participate in the PL that was a part of the ML-PBL study. Her goal of creating an engaging learning environment for her students did not alter but was enhanced by her role as teacher leader.

Opening spaces for teachers to share and learn from each other, honoring the experiences that teachers bring to the table, and supporting the development of a collaborative learning community are at the core of ML-PBL professional learning. Through the sharing of student artifacts, participating in panel discussions, and the purposeful integration of experienced and novice teachers, ML-PBL professional sessions provide many opportunities for teacher leadership. Ms. Butler saw the value in these experiences and the combination of teacher agency, preparation, and opportunity allowed her to support student learning beyond her own classroom.

CHAPTER 11

Lessons Learned from PBL in Science Teaching and Learning

JOSEPH KRAJCIK, EMILY C. ADAH MILLER, AND BARBARA SCHNEIDER

> ML-PBL has changed the lives of these little children. They love science and keep asking, "Is it going to be science today?'" The experiences they are having in science will be in their minds forever, and they will remember it as one of the happiest times they had in school.
>
> —MS. TILSON

> PBL is just my way of life for my teaching now. That's the way all of my teaching is now. It is not specifically just in science anymore. In PBL, you're making kids think about the world around them and think about why things are and why things do this—it's basically all science. This program teaches kids how to think, it teaches you about making them aware of things around them, and questioning why the things around you do what they do: "How can I change things?" I guess it's that basically what the program has done for me is opened up the way I teach.
>
> —MR. STARR

Why do children in the Multiple Literacies in Project-Based Learning (ML-PBL) find their science classes so enjoyable? Why do ML-PBL science classes provide opportunities where children can work with their classmates to figure out and make sense of the world around them, and solve problems they find relevant to their lives? Our answer—based on a wealth of statistical data and in-depth case studies—is that, with ML-PBL, children learn in science environments that deliberately incorporate the principles of project-based learning (PBL).[1] The incorporation of these principles changes the way that teachers think about science learning, as the PBL principles aid them in supporting children in learning not only disciplinary knowledge, but also scientific and engineering practices and crosscutting concepts (such as cause and effect, systems and systems models, and patterns). This transformation cannot be achieved through a new textbook or series of online instructions. Instead, teachers and students need experiences and supports that champion how students learn by doing, take ownership of their ideas, and communicate ideas with their peers and community.

The story of this transformation has been told through numbers, but the words and actions of the students and their teachers in the cases reported in this book, as they unfold in their classroom, breathe life into the mere description.[2] The nine cases describe and exemplify how we can make science learning a central and meaningful experience in the lives of all our students, especially those in the formative stages of their education. All of the cases represent teachers who took part in the ML-PBL study over the course of three years and used PBL to engage diverse student populations in learning science by *doing* science.

Using observations, videos, interviews, and assessments, the cases show how science learning environments can be transformed into ones where elementary school children develop deep knowledge that enables them to make sense of new situations and promote their social and emotional learning. These cases have explored how and why this happens and the extension of such practices to a variety of context and classroom cultures. What are key lessons learned from these case studies? This is not a "how to do it" book—rather, it describes the change in teachers' perspectives as they watch the change in their students and experience the principal ideas of how children learn, are motivated, and are engaged in exploring and understanding their natural world.

CHANGING SCIENCE LEARNING

Transforming science teaching and learning begins by using principles built on the evidence of learning theories: such as how students learn; how to change the direction of a classroom from one in which teachers are being knowledge dispensers to one where students collectively generate new understandings by exploring questions they find meaningful; and how teachers gradually see the value of taking on roles that facilitate this knowledge generation.[3] ML-PBL was developed using critical components of teaching and learning and the ways these relate to bringing about change in student learning. ML-PBL has three central components: (1) high-quality teacher and student materials and experiences that are engaging and advance academic and social and emotional learning (SEL) for all students; (2) professional learning that helps teachers support their students in doing science; and (3) assessments that engage students in performances that build an evidential base of what the students have learned.

ML-PBL provides high-quality teacher and student materials that use the principles of PBL as the framework for designing the classroom experience. Highly developed materials allow teachers and students to use sophisticated science practices and science ideas to make sense of phenomena and solve worthwhile problems. These materials are not scripted, as we recognize that students have different experiences on which teachers need to capitalize. For example, in chapter 9, Luzmaria adapts the ML-PBL curriculum materials to her bilingual third-graders' cultural experiences.

In addition, the ML-PBL materials carefully sequence tasks across time to provide coherence to the learning. Because the nature of the challenge lies within the instructional materials, the materials are scaffolded for the teachers to aid in posing challenging tasks, such as constructing models and generating evidence-based claims.

A professional learning (PL) design that brings forward the PBL principles for teacher learning is a key to the success of ML-PBL. In PL sessions, the facilitators engage the teachers in sensemaking about how to enact PBL by immersing them in the same experiences as their students, but as critical and reflective practitioners. Guided by the PBL principles, these sessions include group collaborations, deep meaningful discussions about teaching, techniques for raising meaningful and relevant questions, generating authentic artifacts, and learning by doing. Each PL day is framed by reviewing prior learning with the teachers, the Driving Question that supports the students in the ML-PBL units, and how they have enabled the students to ask their own questions. One of the major goals of PL is to form a community of teacher learners figuring out problems and constructing shared knowledge to advance their own science practices. In chapter 10, Ms. Butler explains how transformative her own experiences within the

PL were and how they led her to become a facilitator to support other elementary teachers within her district in enacting ML-PBL.

The third system component of ML-PBL is the formative assessments, which afford the students an opportunity to expand their learning by applying it to new problems and situations. In chapters 6 and 7, Ms. Kramer and Ms. Tilson scaffold students in learning to create models that explain phenomena. In Ms. Kramer's case, this is exemplified when, in the post-unit assessment for the Squirrels Unit, students built models to explain the extinction of the stegosaurus during the unit, and then drew models to explain what would happen to the Eastern Gray Squirrels if all the trees were cut down. These formative assessments are the conclusion of the progression of work that the students have built on as they have learned the use of crosscutting concepts—such as patterns, cause and effect, scale, and stability and change—which allow them to build models and apply them to new situations.

These three components of the ML-PBL—high-quality teacher and student learning materials and experiences, PL, and assessments—work together to promote change in classroom environments and foster student learning. The nine cases in this book were deliberately developed to illustrate how the components of the ML-PBL are enacted in the classroom, taking into account supports for SEL, cultural responsiveness, and hands-on experiences for all students. Reviewing the cases, several themes emerged that are described below.

LESSONS LEARNED

Learning to Use the Principles of PBL in ML-PBL

One of the fundamental aspects of PBL is the Driving Question that engages learners and supports them in connecting ideas for understanding phenomena and problem-solving. Using Driving Questions has been shown to be challenging and to take considerable time to master.[4] However, in chapter 2—Mr. Starr's case—we see how he becomes confident in using the Driving Question to connect students' ideas across the year. The Driving Question becomes a tool to help students synthesize and reflect on the corresponding scientific phenomena.

While using the Driving Question to connect ideas is challenging, engaging learners in asking their own questions is even more difficult. Despite these hurdles, in the cases in this book, we see the teachers take these initial steps. In Ms. Butler's case, she comes to learn the value of getting students to ask questions and post them on the Driving Question Board. This also occurs in Ms. Smith's case (chapter 3), where her instructional changes across the year show how she learned to support her students in figuring out phenomena and the value in having them become independent learners. What is perhaps one of the key takeaways for the teachers using the Driving Questions Board is that, although slightly anxiety-inducing and intellectually demanding, consistent use over time—not just one lesson, one week, or even one unit—creates learning environments that position students as independent learners.

Supporting Students in Developing Social and Emotional Learning

Chapter 1 describes how ML-PBL fosters SEL in three important domains: ownership, self-reflection, and collaboration.[5] By asking their own questions and posting them on the Driving Question Board, learners develop ownership of their ideas, which motivates and engages them in challenging work like building models. Throughout the unit, the students are directed to return to the questions they have asked, positioning them as responsible for their own learning. This is most evident in Ms. Smith's class, where she continuously pushes her students to return to their questions and find new ways of answering them, both individually and collectively.

Building artifacts also supports students' ownership and self-reflection. During the Birds Unit in Luzmaria's class, after the students learned how local birds thrive, they realized that their own cultural practice of using dye to color baby chicks' feathers is harmful. The self-reflection that they engaged in regarding the chicks' plight encouraged them to find ways to protect the chicks and educate their community about the practice through identifying a problem, creating a solution, and developing an artifact together. In this case, the students created posters warning about the harm of using coloring dye on the chicks—here, the students empathized with the threats to the chicks' survival, made the problem their own, and worked collaboratively with their classmates on an artifact to protect the chicks.

In building artifacts, students must also collaborate together: a critical part of developing SEL skills. As seen in Ms. Smith's class, the third-graders design and built a bird feeder. As they collaborate, students develop communication and relationship skills important for SEL. This is also seen when students build models, such as those we see in the cases presented in this book. In this process, students reflect on whether their model provides an explanation for the event under study and whether it takes into consideration the evidence collected. Focusing on how the model can explain the phenomenon with sufficient evidence promotes students' skill of self-reflection as well as ownership of their learning, when providing arguments and evidence for their models.

Supporting Students in Scientific Thinking

Supporting students to think critically across time promotes the scientific thinking necessary for problem-solving and making sense of phenomena. Using evidence to support claims, building models, and using the lens of systems thinking are examples of three fundamental scientific thinking skills. Systems thinking is key to solving problems because it focuses learners on identifying important components in a system and describing the relationships among those components. When students construct models, they need to first identify all the components of the model, then describe the relationships between the components, and finally decide if those relationships explain the phenomena under investigation. The ML-PBL units support the careful development of these scientific thinking skills across the four third-grade units. We see this development in Ms. Kramer's and Ms. Tilson's classes, in which the development of systems thinking and modeling is scaffolded from concrete to more complex abstract situations.

The ML-PBL materials also help in establishing the competency of supporting claims using evidence across the four units in the third grade. Evidence is introduced in the Squirrels Unit with the following support: "I have seen evidence or others have seen this evidence which backs up my claims that helps squirrels survive." The importance of claims being supported by evidence is also developed in Luzmaria's case when she introduces the use of "whispers" to call out the distinguishing concept of evidence. What is particularly culturally relevant about using these "evidence whispers" is that, in her students' families, whispering is viewed as a mechanism marking a special event at home. Signaling whispering for evidence at school, coupled by its value at home, establishes not only the unique value of evidence but its connection to the students' cultural identity.

Using Collaboration and Discourse Moves to Support Sensemaking

Engaging children in discourse to build shared knowledge with one another is a key feature of PBL. The ML-PBL lessons are rich with suggested discourse prompts and suggested open-ended questions that use discourse moves to support teachers in promoting sensemaking.[6] These practices are also highlighted in PL sessions specifically focused on demonstrating the use of teacher discourse moves in the classroom and understanding the teacher's role as discussion facilitator.

In Mr. Starr's case, he progresses from the first unit on squirrels to the third unit on plants by asking more pressing questions in relation to the Driving Question. Mr. Starr has come to learn how to use discourse moves to deepen student reasoning, clarify their thinking, and make students' ideas public. In a typical non-ML-PBL classroom, the teacher asks a question, the students respond, and the teacher then evaluates the response. In ML-PBL units and PL, teachers are encouraged to purposefully disrupt this structure: they not only develop the capacity to deepen students' responses and leverage their ideas, but they also engage students in each other's thinking by having them respond to each other. For this to be effective, teachers have to help students shift their mind-set to one where they value an idea as important for the group's knowledge-building process.

For example, if a student expresses an idea that might be scientifically problematic, another student tries to understand where the ideas are coming from, and then a third attempts to connect the idea to a previous idea or to the investigation. The students are in control of making connections between one another. No idea is to be discredited, but instead is seen as a springboard for more exploration. Another discourse move is related to the teacher helping students deepen their reasoning. For example, a teacher might respond to a student's idea by asking them to say more about the thinking process that led to their claim. The teacher might ask the student to show the class their evidence. This places the importance on the process and not simply the outcome. Often, the students' reasoning may be missing key steps, but a slight nudge could lead students to further discovery. In addition, providing evidence and a rationale allows other students to build on the evidence, make slight adjustments, and come to new conclusions. Both of these moves are important in establishing a classroom environment in which students work collaboratively to engage in sensemaking and knowledge-building.

Integrating Experiences with Literacy

As the name implies, Multiple Literacies in Project-Based Learning integrates various literacy competencies—reading, writing, speaking, listening, representing, and viewing—with students' experiences. The design of the materials in ML-PBL purposefully integrates literacy with experiences. This is apparent in chapter 4, where Ms. Lane engages students in observing and investigating water squirters and the Super Soaker before they engage in texts about the development of the Super Soaker. The ML-PBL materials and PL promote making connections between students' lived experiences in the school and the community and the texts. Many of the readings in ML-PBL were purposefully designed to make these links clear.

In Ms. Lane's case, she supports students in making connections between the science texts and the designs of their toys. This approach to integrating meaningful literacy with experiences contrasts with traditional approaches in which students read about science and natural phenomena in the absence of personally related experiences. This approach to literacy integration in science instruction promotes students in developing more useful knowledge where they explore the text in order to get more insight into their own experiences and observations. Texts, similar to their classmates' ideas, help students to establish evidence and build on what they have already discovered through their process of inquiry.

The integration of ML-PBL practices can also be found in other subjects taught by the teachers, such as mathematics and social studies. The case of Ms. Hegg (chapter 8) shows how she adapts questioning and other scientific practices into her teaching of all her subjects over the course of the entire day. ML-PBL also specifically features mathematics, with students measuring, estimating, and comparing patterns of animal growth; the distances a car travels with a given force; and constructing bird feeders. Across other subjects, the integration of science is valuable, as the three dimensions of learning are essential for promoting knowledge acquisition in any field. However, science is often given less time, attention, and understanding in many elementary classrooms. One of the most critical recommendations of this work is the importance of elevating science alongside reading and mathematics as essential skills of twenty-first century learning.

Enhancing the Teaching of PBL with Technology

Although not necessary, the use of technology can enhance the use of ML-PBL in the teaching and learning of science. Ms. Lawson's case (chapter 5) provides valuable insights into the use of technology. She incorporates the use of a simulation tool to support students' learning of a challenging performance expectation from the Next Generation Science Standards: understanding the role of balanced and unbalanced forces. The force and motion simulation from PhET provides students with an interactive visual where they can quickly make predictions and observe what happens.[7] Another technology tool, *Flipbook*, allows users to develop computer-based models.[8] The advantage of using *Flipbook* to develop models over pencil and paper models is that learners can simulate (i.e., run) a model, allowing learners to judge if their model is behaving as expected. When addressing literacy in the classroom, *WeRead* provides tools that can support learners in the comprehension of the text—these tools include a dictionary and a text reader.[9] However, although technology can enhance students' learning in PBL, it is not a necessity. As stated by Ms. Lane, educational technology cannot replace the teacher.

While the use of video does not replace authentic experience, it can enhance ML-PBL. ML-PBL promotes students engaging in firsthand experiences of phenomena, but this approach is not always feasible: there are times when the technology can provide experiences that would be impossible for most students to experience. In the Birds Unit, students conduct fieldwork to gather observational data about the birds that live near their school, asking their own questions based on their observations. However, at times in the unit, there are some experiences that are better observed on video, if not impossible to get firsthand—for example, observing the hunting behavior of a hawk. In these instances, the use of video coupled with firsthand experience can give the student a fuller picture of the world.

Connecting Assessment and Learning

Above, we have noted the importance of the formative assessment process used in the ML-PBL units. Given at the end of each unit, these post-unit assessments are used to evaluate the students' ability to figure out phenomena or solve a scientific problem, not to repeat a memorized fact. These solutions show their relevance by being connected to the students' own lives and help them realize the importance of the phenomena under investigation—for example, why certain animals survive and others do not. The emphasis here is on having the students use their new ability in using disciplinary core ideas, scientific practices, and crosscutting concepts to form claims based on evidence, construct a model and produce an artifact that responds to the Driving Question. One of the most encouraging benefits of ML-PBL is found in Ms. Tilson's class, which, at the beginning of the school year, had a very large percentage of struggling readers, minority students, and those with limited social and economic resources. Yet the students took to ML-PBL with an enthusiasm and used it as an opportunity to show their thoughts by constructing models and their assessment scores.

Developing Teacher Leaders and Forming Relationships with School Administrators

There are two other important messages that have surfaced from the implementation of the ML-BPL project. The first is the importance of developing teacher leaders who can organize vibrant science communities in their schools. The second is the importance of developing strong partnerships with school administrators, science directors, teachers, and community members to facilitate the implementation of ML-PBL in their schools and districts.

With respect to developing teacher leaders, in ML-PBL, the PL experiences rely on the expertise of practicing professionals who have acquired an interest and expertise in implementing the projects. These teacher leaders have an unusual place in our work, as they help to review unit lessons, offer suggestions on experiences, support new teachers interested in using ML-PBL, and establish science communities in their schools and districts. They also form connections with families and other community groups, reinforcing the value of science learning and its accessibility to students not just within but also outside of school. This outreach to parents reinforces the ideas of relevance and cultural community responsiveness that are essential for helping students understand the value of learning science and tackling science-related events impacting the health and well-being of their community: for example, contaminated water supplies, eroding shorelines, and the growing amount of wildlife at risk. It is also the case that some of our teacher leaders have become leaders in their districts and raised the awareness of creating a stronger pipeline for students interested in pursuing STEM careers.

Few interventions can be sustained in a school district without the support and encouragement of school administrators. The ML-PBL team has consistently recognized the importance of establishing trusting relationships with district leaders, and many of these leaders have been critical in assisting the team in accessing schools, providing opportunities for PL, and working with us to promote the NGSS performance expectations. Although working with administrators is of the utmost importance, it is sometimes unstable, particularly in urban areas because of retention practices. Principals and superintendents frequently change, and their replacements often do not see the value and importance of science as experiential learning and instead turn to programs that rely primarily on traditional science textbooks. We have worked assiduously toward keeping our administrators informed about our program's successes and opportunities for sustainability—and have worked with them to communicate these messages to larger state and national groups.

CONCLUDING THOUGHTS

Our work has shown that science can be especially valuable for all students, even struggling readers. Opportunities like conducting experiments and drawing models can be a gateway for learners who need other forms of instructions for acquiring knowledge. We have deliberately over-sampled students who have limited social and economic resources, members of minority racial and ethnic groups, and students with special needs. Our case studies and quantitative research shows that ML-PBL is successful among all students.[10]

Scholars and policy makers are often somewhat skeptical of the generalizability of case studies, even those conducted with the highest standards of scholarship. However, in this instance, the purposive selection of these case study teachers—from a generalizable random sample of schools and students—reflects some of the critical features of ML-PBL and their impact on student academic and SEL. These case studies are supported by the evidence provided in the ML-PBL efficacy study, which shows the effectiveness of ML-PBL across our school sites as well as the generalizability of these findings to the nation as a whole.[11]

Although implementing ML-PBL is challenging, especially when getting started and beginning the development of the questioning process among students, the results—as Ms. Tilson says—are "life-changing." This is because the intervention fosters students to become active learners in their classrooms, figuring out phenomena, and problem-solving. ML-PBL students come to understand the elements of human survival, balanced and unbalanced forces, differences between species, and the ecosystem of which they are a part. They can draw cause and effect models, provide explanations, use a systems perspective to make sense of problems, and work together in groups, respecting, listening, and supporting each other. These are competencies that it is often assumed cannot be mastered by third graders, but that underestimates the power of young children when given the freedom to learn by "doing science" in principled and strategically crafted engaging science environments.

APPENDIX A

Third-Grade Multiple Literacies in Project-Based Learning Units Summaries

UNIT 3.1 SQUIRRELS/ADAPTATION

In unit 3.1, the Driving Question is *Why do I see so many squirrels but can't find any stegosauruses?* The students examine the life of a squirrel, and develop an intimate picture of how it survives outside. Students are expected to draw their first models and make claims that are supported by evidence; they participate in their first fieldwork, use observations notes to track what they see; and they develop initial understandings of what it means to engage in academic discourse. Additionally, the young third-graders are also starting to figure out how to work with partners and in small groups, developing and presenting their shared artifacts.

In the first Learning Set, students observe squirrels in their community. They conduct investigations about how the squirrels might find food and water outside and how they protect themselves from predators. The class develops a shared systems model that explains how squirrels interact with other organisms—such as oak trees, spiders, and hawks—in their environment. By exploring the Driving Question, students learn that each animal and plant meets its needs for survival. Students consider the importance of specific structures and characteristics that relate to the squirrels' survival. They develop an understanding that structures can be examined to gain insight into how an animal or plant might live and the characteristics of the ecosystem in which they live. This understanding is crucial for students to make sense of how scientists use fossils to recreate scenarios related to ancient animals, plants, and their ecosystems. They compare prehistoric structures revealed in fossils with present-day structures. They also analyze fossils of prehistoric animals to consider why, when the environment changes (such as when a food source disappears), some animals will survive while other animals will not be able to meet their needs and die. For the final artifact, students create a model to explain that, as the environment changed 150 million years ago, some animals (early mammals) were able to adapt and others (the stegosaurus) died out. They expand the model in writing (in a short story) or act it out (in a drama presentation). The expectation is that students can explain that species that survive hundreds of millions of years do so because they are either very adaptable to changes in the environment or have wide diversity among them.

UNIT 3.2 TOYS/FORCES AND MOTION

The Driving Question for unit 3.2 is *How can we design fun moving toys that any kid can build?* Here, third-graders enjoy playing with toys and creating them. Most of the toys that students play with are carefully engineered by a group of adults for specific purposes, down to the final and most minute detail. However, in this unit, students engineer their own toys while continuing to concentrate on developing models and paying increased attention to the need for evidence to support scientific claims. They also continue to hone the practices of discourse: sharing ideas, listening to others, and comparing different ideas.

To answer the Driving Question for unit 3.2, the students start by experiencing toy rockets—both a large rocket shown to the entire class and smaller rockets that the students can explore. Students try to predict the motion of the rockets as the toys launch into the air and come down, as well as explain what caused them to start and stop moving. They engage with the science ideas of forces, both balanced and unbalanced, and patterns of motion. Students also work with other students in a small group to interview a kindergartener to make plans to develop the toy according to the kindergartener's specifications.

In this unit, students make prototypes of moving toys, then observe and develop models to describe the pattern of motion they detected. They work with a toy boat, a car, and a rocket made out of a bottle to draw a model of the forces involved in the movement of the toys and also to show that the forces can be used to explain and predict patterns of motion. Next, the students use ideas of forces to explain how magnets and electrical attractions work. The unit culminates in a toy design that can either stop suddenly, pick up speed, or slow down, according to the request of the kindergartener who was interviewed at the beginning. Each student group must present their toy to the larger group and explain how its design works to accomplish the movement goal. The final artifact is a design portfolio that collects the investigations about the effects of balanced and unbalanced forces and contact and non-contact forces on the motion of the toys built, investigated, and redesigned throughout the unit.

UNIT 3.3 BIRDS/BIODIVERSITY

Unit 3.3, whose Driving Question is *How can we help the birds near our school grow up and thrive?*, starts in February, when the only birds that students will likely see are overwintering birds. Over the course of the unit, as they go outside to look for birds with binoculars, the students gradually see birds like robins, bluebirds, and finches return. The migration of birds and bird behavior is something that students have also seen as the seasons change. But the third-graders are astounded to learn that migration is a bird behavior that is recalled. Student also learn about how the life cycle is a process that both has similarities across species and is related to the survival of a species.

In exploring the Driving Question, the students conduct fieldwork to gather observational data about the birds that live near the school and ask their own questions to explore based on their observations. They make claims that the birds have behavioral traits that contribute to their chance to survive. They witness birds foraging for food and make a claim about the food the birds might eat, and the availability of that food in the environment by the school. Together, they conduct a resource inventory and organize data to argue that some necessary resources are not available. Each student group focuses on a chosen bird; based on what the bird eats and relies on to thrive, they write a problem related to the resources of which a bird might need more. The students use the birds' behaviors and life cycles as well as the phenological changes in the area to develop a solution to the problem that will enable some birds to meet their needs and thrive.

In the final Learning Set, students put the finishing touches on a plan to design bird feeders. The groups present their bird feeders to the community and explain how they took into account the physical and behavioral traits of their focus bird, its life cycle and changing need(s), the features of the environment, and the resources the bird feeder supplies that may be lacking in the environment near the school. The students are able to consider where to place the bird feeders, and they check on their feeders to see if any animals—hopefully, birds—made use of it. Students ultimately explain how local birds, especially native birds, should be protected.

UNIT 3.4 PLANTS/WEATHER/CLIMATE

In Unit 3.4, students explore the Driving Question, *How can we plan gardens in our community to grow plants for food?* This unit revisits scientific ideas from earlier units, including life cycle, adaptation with more sophistication, and new ideas about climate and weather. The unit takes advantage of the spring weather to involve students in growing plants inside and then planting them in an outdoor plot. They transplant beans and other vegetables after they have investigated the weather conditions and determined that they can support their seedlings.

The unit is centered on a problem of severe weather, such as flooding, and challenges students to develop a solution that will mitigate the effects of the hazardous weather. Students spend the first few weeks looking at maps and determining that some environmental conditions are ideal for some plants and not others. They learn about apples, corn, and other crops. At the same time, there are ongoing investigations about how plants germinate, and how they have predictable life cycles with some of the same—and some different—stages as the birds that they studied in the Birds Unit. Finally, the students learn about flooding and frost and meet an engineer who developed a solution to grow apples even when there are unexpected cold conditions. Students consider their local area and learn about what local scientists have done to protect plants from hazardous weather.

In this final unit, students learn to ask scientific questions; make quantitative observations; investigate plants and weather using texts, maps, and graphs; and develop systems models of how plants' traits affect their survival. Students select a plant to grow for their garden based on what will grow in the space they have and what the community might be able to use. The final artifact includes planning and designing a garden and making claims about the merits of a solution, tool, or process to protect the plants from weather-related hazards or changes in the environment. Ultimately, the students harvest and deliver the food to families and community members in need.

APPENDIX B

Anatomy of an ML-PBL Lesson

The curriculum for each grade level consists of four units of instruction, each framed by a Driving Question and an anchoring phenomenon, and each culminating in a final artifact (see table B.1).

Unit-Level Features

- Unit Driving Question (DQ)
- Enduring Understanding Statements
- Generalizations
- Overarching Phenomenon
- Final Artifact
- Primary and Secondary NGSS PEs
- Embedded Applications of CCSS—ELA/Literacy, CCSS—Mathematics
- Featured Social and Emotional Learning (SEL) and Equity Goals

Units are subdivided into Learning Sets framed by questions that build toward the unit DQ.

The Unit Table of Contents provides an overview of the Learning Set and Lesson DQs.

Unit Learning Progression Charts provide a visual overview

Lesson design features provide coherence within and across lessons and units.

- Three-Dimensional Learning Performance Statements
- Figuring Out Statements
- Look Fors (Formative Assessment Guidance)
- Discourse Moves
- Lesson Artifact
- Evidence Statements

TABLE B.1 Driving Questions, phenomena, and artifacts for third-grade units

	ML-PBL UNIT 3.1	ML-PBL UNIT 3.2	ML-PBL UNIT 3.3	ML-PBL UNIT 3.4
Driving Question	*Why do I see so many squirrels but can't find any stegosauruses?*	*How can we design fun moving toys that any kid can build?*	*How can we help the birds near our school grow up and thrive?*	*How can we plan gardens in our community to grow plants for food?*
Phenomenon	Animals meet their needs to survive in their environment in different ways.	Different forces make toys move.	Many birds migrate in flocks.	Engineers design spaces to grow plants all over the world and in hazardous weather.
Artifact	Students develop a play, story, or model of how the stegosaurus did not survive and the *eutheria* did survive.	Students build a toy according to the specifications of a kindergartener.	Students design and build a bird feeder for a local species of birds.	Students grow plants for their community and plan for protecting the plants from flooding.

The Driving Question (DQ). The DQ occurs at three levels: the unit level, the Learning Set level, and the lesson level. The Driving Questions gradually and purposefully move students toward using the three dimensions of the Next Generation Science Standards (NGSS) to explain and predict the anchoring phenomenon in the unit. The Driving Questions are nested to reinforce coherence. All lesson-level Driving Questions can be understood as answering the Learning Set Driving Question and, in turn, the unit-level Driving Question.

Learning Performance Statement (LP). Each Learning Set (LS) and each lesson has a three-dimensional learning performance (LP)—a 3D learning goal. The LP is assessed at the Look For level (an informal assessment—what the teacher is looking for and "noticing") and the Evidence Statement level (which describes the lesson product as an artifact of the LP [i.e., the final model, the analysis of the data, or the claim]).

Building Toward PEs. Throughout the unit, students are building toward meeting a bundle of NGSS Performance Expectations (PEs). Each lesson focuses on building toward one or more PEs, which are listed below the lesson LP.

Figuring Out Statements. Figuring Out Statements reflect the DCI elements with respect to their interaction with the phenomenon and with the Driving Question. They represent the heavy cognitive lifting of sensemaking expected of the students. We define *scientific sensemaking* as the dialogic activity of searching for meaning and coherence using scientific and engineering ideas and practices for explaining phenomena and solving problems.

Look For Statements. Look For Statements support the collaborative nature of the practices and/or the crosscutting concepts (CCCs) with respect both to the co-creation of cultural practices and to the lesson-level LP. They signal what the students should be doing and the (CCC) lenses they should be using as they work together in figuring out and sensemaking. Look Fors also provide guidance for formative assessment—what the teacher is looking for, "noticing," and prompting for.

Evidence Statements. Evidence Statements provide a description of the tangible/observable product of the lesson. The Evidence Statement links back to the LP and specifies clearly what should be considered/observed as evidence that students have met the LP (the learning goal of the lesson).

Formative Assessment Opportunities. Both Look Fors and Evidence Statements provide guidance for assessing student progress toward learning goals.

Discourse Moves (WIDA Resources). The discourse moves, developed by the Wisconsin Center for Educational Research (WIDA), respond to the call in the English Language Proficiency Development (ELPD) Framework for supporting the language of doing science.[1] Social and emotional learning (SEL) practices describe analytic tasks, receptive and productive functions, or cognitive and linguistic demands that are delineated in the science and engineering practices (combined with the CCCs and DCIs) of the NGSS. The discourse moves support all of the purposes of engaging in these practices through discourse.

For example, after a student expresses an idea while engaging in modeling, the discourse move "Help students clarify an idea" means that the teacher would ask questions seeking to make the student's language more specific and better convey their idea; thus, both linguistic and cognitive demands are supported—and the purposes of expressing the idea are accomplished.

Embedded Language Supports. Throughout the ML-PBL units, language supports (support for language acquisition) are embedded as part and parcel of engaging in the three dimensions of the NGSS and as referenced in NGSS Appendix D, the ELDP Framework, and current research and recommendations in EL Education. The most important feature is ML-PBL's integrated and inclusive design approach to ELs. This feature involves maintaining high expectations for ELs, enhanced opportunity for negotiation of meaning as part of situated contexts of science, and focusing on students' ideas and understandings from a sensemaking stance. That is, we take the stance that all students' ideas are useful for collective knowledge-building, and through embedded informal assessments, the teacher describes students' ideas as productive. When students who are learning English are motivated to learn science and viewed by others—especially the teacher—from a resource-rich perspective, their performance as language and disciplinary content learners elevates.

SEL/Equity Goals. The goals, comprising part of the lesson-level LP, are reflected in the Look Fors and are based on current research. As students engage in the NGSS, the sociocultural dimension of the science practices (collaboration, negotiating group and power dynamics, and supporting relationships and self-concept) can be furthered at the same time through purposeful scaffolding.

APPENDIX C

ML-PBL Time in Professional Learning

Table C.1 shows the number of hours ML-PBL teachers spent on professional learning (PL). Overall, among the formal scheduled PL sessions, each treatment teacher received approximately seven days of formal scheduled PL sessions (counting in-person and formal virtual hours) throughout the school year.

TABLE C.1 Time spent in professional learning

DATE	HOURS	TYPE
Summer		
• August 2018	3 days, 7 hours each	Face-to-face
School year		
• November 2018–April 2019	3 days, 7 hours each	Face-to-face
• November 2018–April 2019	3 days, 1 hour each	Virtual
Total	45 hours	

Notes

Chapter 1

1. This work is supported by the George Lucas Educational Research Foundation. All opinions are those of the authors and not the George Lucas Educational Research Foundation.
2. Because this is a book about the teaching of science at the third-grade level, the idea that science learning consists of making sense of phenomena is used frequently. Here, "phenomena" is understood to mean natural events that can be observed more than once and are repeatable.
3. See National Research Council, *A Framework for K–12 Science Education: Practices, Crosscutting Concepts, and Core Ideas* (Washington, DC: National Academies Press, 2012); National Research Council, *Education for Life and Work: Developing Transferable Knowledge and Skills in the 21st Century* (Washington, DC: National Academies Press, 2012).
4. See John Dewey, *The School and Society: Dewey on Education* (New York: Teachers College Press, 1938).
5. See Marie Baines et al., "Why Is Social and Emotional Learning Essential to Project-Based Learning?" (LER position paper 2, George Lucas Educational Foundation, San Rafael, California, 2017); and Barbara Condliffe et al., *Project-Based Learning: A Literature Review* (New York: MDRC, 2016).
6. We refer to the *Why do I see so many squirrels but can't find any stegosauruses?* unit as the "Squirrels Unit." This is our approach for the "Toys Unit," the "Birds Unit," and the "Plants Unit" as well.
7. See Joseph S. Krajcik and Namsoo Shin, "Project-Based Learning," in *The Cambridge Handbook of the Learning Sciences*, ed. R. Keith Sawyer (New York: Cambridge University Press, 2014), 275–297; and Joseph S. Krajcik and Charlene M. Czerniak, *Teaching Science in Elementary and Middle School Classrooms: A Project-Based Learning Approach*, 5th ed. (New York: Routledge, 2018).
8. *Disciplinary core ideas* are what the NRC's *Framework for K–12 Science Education* identifies as necessary to explain a host of phenomena. The other two features are science and engineering practices and crosscutting concepts.
9. See National Research Council, *Framework for K–12 Science Education*. See also reform documents from Finland, Germany, and PISA: Finnish National Board of Education (FNBE), *National Core Curriculum for General Upper Secondary Schools 2015* (Helsinki: Finnish National Board of Education (FNBE), 2015). Retrieved from http://www.oph.fi/saadokset_ja_ohjeet/opetussuunnitelmien_ja_tutkintojen_perusteet/lukiokoulutus/lops2016/103/0/lukion_opetussuunnitelman_perusteet_2015; Christoph Kulgemeyer and Horst Schecker, "Research on Educational Standards in German Science Education—Towards a Model of Student Competences," *EURASIA Journal of Mathematics, Science & Technology Education* 10, no. 4 (2014): 257–269, doi:10.12973/eurasia.2014.1081a; and OECD, *PISA 2015 Assessment and Analytical Framework: Science, Reading, Mathematic and Financial Literacy* (Paris: OECD Publishing, 2016).

10. See National Research Council, *How People Learn: Brain, Mind, Experience, and School* (Washington, DC: National Academies Press, 1999); National Research Council, *Taking Science to School: Learning and Teaching Science in Grades K–8* (Washington, DC: National Academies Press, 2007); R. Keith Sawyer, ed., *The Cambridge Handbook of the Learning Sciences*, 2nd ed. (New York: Cambridge, 2014); Krajcik and Shin, "Project-Based Learning"; and Emily C. Miller and Joseph Krajcik, "Promoting Deep Learning Through Project-Based Learning: A Design Problem," *Disciplinary and Interdisciplinary Science Education Research* 1, no. 7 (2019).
11. See National Research Council, *Framework for K–12 Science Education*; and NGSS Lead States, *Next Generation Science Standards* (Washington, DC: National Academies Press, 2013).
12. See National Research Council, *Education for Life and Work.*
13. See National Research Council, *Framework for K–12 Science Education.*
14. Three-dimensional learning is often written as "3D learning."
15. See Ravit Duncan, Joseph Krajcik, and Ann Rivet, eds. *Disciplinary Core Ideas: Reshaping Teaching and Learning* (Arlington, VA: National Science Teachers Association Press, 2016).
16. See Jeffrey Nordine and Okhee Lee, eds., *Crosscutting Concepts: Strengthening Science and Engineering Learning* (Arlington, VA: National Science Teaching Association Press, 2021).
17. See Christine Schwartz, Cynthia Passmore, and Brian Reiser, eds., *Helping Students Make Sense of the World Using Next Generation Science and Engineering Practices* (Arlington, VA: National Science Teaching Association Press, 2017).
18. See Carol L. Smith et al., "Implications of Research on Children's Learning for Standards and Assessment: A Proposed Learning Progression for Matter and the Atomic Molecular Theory," *Measurement: Interdisciplinary Research and Perspectives* 4, no. 1–2: 1–98, doi:10.1080/15366367.2006.9678570; and National Research Council, *Taking Science to School.*
19. Robert J. Jagers, Deborah Rivas-Drake, and Teresa Borowski, "Equity and Social and Emotional Learning: A Cultural Analysis," *Frameworks Briefs, Special Issues Series* (2018), 1–17; and Joseph A. Durlak et al., eds., *Handbook of Social and Emotional Learning: Research and Practice* (New York: Guilford Publications, 2015).
20. Although this book focuses on enactments of ML-PBL in the third grade, we have also created units for fourth and fifth grades. All materials for third, fourth, and fifth grades can be found and downloaded at: https://sprocket.lucasedresearch.org/.
21. For more information on evidence-centered design, see Christopher J. Harris et al., "Designing Knowledge-In-Use Assessments to Promote Deeper Learning," *Educational Measurement: Issues and Practice* 38, no. 2 (2019): 53–67, doi:10.1111/emip.12253; and Robert J. Mislevy and Geneva D. Haertel, "Implications of Evidence-Centered Design for Educational Testing," *Educational Measurement: Issues and Practice* 25, no. 4 (2006): 6–20, doi:10.1111/j.1745-3992.2006.00075.x.
22. Joseph Krajcik et al., *Assessing the Effect of Project-Based Learning on Science Learning in Elementary Schools* (technical report, George Lucas Foundation, San Rafael, California, 2020).
23. See Christopher J. Harris et al., "Impact of Project-Based Curriculum Materials on Student Learning in Science: Results of a Randomized Controlled Trial," *Journal of Research in Science Teaching* 52, no. 10 (2015): 1362–1385, doi:10.1002/tea.21263; Sharon J. Lynch, Curtis Pyke, and Bonnie H. Grafton, "A Retrospective View of a Study of Middle School Science Curriculum Materials: Implementation, Scale-Up, and Sustainability in Changing Policy Environment," *Journal of Research in Science Teaching* 49, no. 3 (2012): 305–332, doi:10.1002/tea.21000; and Christopher D. Wilson et al., "The Relative Effects and Equity

of Inquiry-Based and Commonplace Science Teaching on Students' Knowledge, Reasoning, and Argumentation," *Journal of Research in Science Teaching* 47, no. 3 (2010): 276–301, doi:10.1002/tea.20329.

24. Gloria Ladson-Billings, "Toward a Theory of Culturally Relevant Pedagogy," *American Educational Research Journal* 32, no. 3 (1995): 465–491, doi:10.3102/00028312032003465.

Chapter 2

1. For more information about the role and importance of using Driving Questions in PBL, see Joseph S. Krajcik and Namsoo Shin, "Project-Based Learning," in *The Cambridge Handbook of the Learning Sciences*, ed. R. Keith Sawyer (New York: Cambridge University Press, 2014), 275–297.
2. For more information about how discourse moves support students' participation and engagement during their science learning process, see Rita MacDonald, Sarah Lord, and Emily Miller, *Teaching the Content Areas to English Language Learners in Secondary Schools* (Cham, Switzerland: Springer, 2019).
3. For more information about the role of revoicing students' ideas as a form of discourse moves to support student sensemaking, see Miranda S. Fitzgerald and Annemarie S. Palincsar, "Teaching Practices That Support Student Sensemaking Across Grades and Disciplines: A Conceptual Review," *Review of Research in Education* 43, no. 1 (2019): 227–248, doi:10.3102/0091732X18821115.
4. For a description of how multimodal representations benefit science learning, see Kok-sing Tang, Cesar Delgado, and Elizabeth B. Moje, "An Integrative Framework for the Analysis of Multiple and Multimodal Representations for Meaning Making in Science Education," *Science Education* 98, no. 2 (2014): 305–326, doi:10.1002/sce.21099.

Chapter 3

1. AnnMarie Baines, *Why Is Social and Emotional Learning Essential to Project-Based Learning?* (LER position paper 2, George Lucas Educational Foundation, San Rafael, California, 2017).
2. Steven R. Covey, *The 7 Habits of Highly Effective People: Powerful Lessons in Personal Change* (New York: Simon & Schuster, 2014).
3. Barbara Schneider et al., "Investigating Optimal Learning Moments in US and Finnish Science Classes," *Journal of Research in Science Teaching* 53 (2016): 400–421, doi:10.1002/tea.21306.
4. Nicole Uphold and Melissa Hudson, "Student-Focused Planning," in *Evidence-Based Instructional Strategies for Transition*, ed. David W. Test (Baltimore: Paul H. Brookes, 2012), 55–78.
5. Collaborative for Academic, Social, and Emotional Learning, *2013 CASEL Guide: Effective Social and Emotional Learning Programs—Preschool and Elementary School Edition* (Chicago: Collaborative for Academic, Social, and Emotional Learning, 2012).
6. Ibid.
7. David Osher et al., "Advancing the Science and Practice of Social and Emotional Learning: Looking Back and Moving Forward," *Review of Research in Education* 40, no. 1 (2016): 644–681, doi:10.3102/0091732X16673595.

Chapter 4

1. For descriptions of examples, opportunities, and obstacles of integrating language literacy and science instruction, see National Research Council, *Literacy for Science: Exploring the*

Intersections of the Next Generation Science Standards and the Common Core for ELA Standards, A Workshop Summary (Washington, DC: National Academies Press, 2014); Annemarie S. Palincsar, "The Next Generation Science Standards and the Common Core State Standards: Proposing a Happy Marriage," *Science and Children* 51, no. 1 (2013): 10–15, doi:10.2505/4/sc13_051_01_10; and P. David Pearson, Elizabeth Moje, and Cynthia Greenleaf, "Literacy and Science: Each in Service of the Other," *Science* 328, no. 5977 (2010): 459–463, doi:10.1126/science.1182595.

2. For more information about the roles of authentic experience and explicit instruction in learning to read and write, see Victoria Purcell-Gates, Nell K. Duke, and Joseph A. Martineau, "Learning to Read and Write Genre-Specific Text: Roles of Authentic Experience and Explicit Teaching," *Reading Research Quarterly* 42, no. 1 (2007): 8–45, doi:10.1598/RRQ.42.1.1
3. For a description of how making connections benefits learning see National Research Council, *How People Learn: Brain, Mind, Experience, and School* (Washington, DC: National Academies Press, 2000).
4. For descriptions of vocabulary instructional practices and different types of vocabulary words commonly used in vocabulary instruction literature, see Isabel L. Beck, Margaret G. McKeown, and Linda Kucan, *Bringing Words to Life: Robust Vocabulary Instruction* (New York: Guilford Press, 2002).
5. For more information about how teachers create coherence in integrated instruction by linking materials, experiences, and contexts, see John T. Guthrie et al., "Influences of Concept-Oriented Reading Instruction on Strategy Use and Conceptual Learning from Text," *Elementary School Journal* 99, no. 4 (1999): 343–366, doi:10.1037/0022-0663.90.2.261.
6. Purcell-Gates, Duke, and Martineau, "Learning to Read and Write Genre-Specific Text."

Chapter 5

1. Most of the technologies described in this case were designed by Elliot Soloway and the "Collabrify" team at the University of Michigan and can be accessed at https://techtransfer.umich.edu/companies/collabrify-it/. The simulation was designed by PhET and can be accessed at https://phet.colorado.edu/. All technologies described in this case are open access.
2. For more about supporting all students to access ideas productive to their thinking, see Annemarie Sullivan Palincsar and Barbara G. Ladewski, "Literacy and the Learning Sciences," in *The Cambridge Handbook of the Learning Sciences*, ed. R. Keith Sawyer (New York: Cambridge University Press, 2006), 299–317.
3. For more about advantages of typing over handwriting, see Steve Graham, Karen R. Harris, and Tanya Santangelo, "Research-Based Writing Practices and the Common Core: Meta-Analysis and Meta-Synthesis," *Elementary School Journal* 115, no. 4 (2015): 498–522, doi:10.1086/681964.
4. The force and motion simulation is available at: https://phet.colorado.edu/en/simulation/forces-and-motion-basics.
5. In the previous lesson, the students were introduced to newtons as a measure of force. Ms. Lawson made it clear that completely understanding newtons was not an expectation in third-grade science. Her discussion of newtons was brief and centered around the idea that higher numbers of newtons indicated that the figure was pulling harder.
6. For the principal tenets of PBL, see Phyllis C. Blumenfeld et al., "Motivating Project-Based Learning: Sustaining the Doing, Supporting the Learning," *Educational Psychologist* 26, no. 3–4 (1991): 369–398, doi:10.1207/s15326985ep2603&4_8.

7. For benefits of curricula including both simulations and hands-on learning experiences, see Tomi Jaakkola, Sami Nurmi, and Koen Veermans, "A Comparison of Students' Conceptual Understanding of Electric Circuits in Simulation Only and Simulation-Laboratory Contexts," *Journal of Research in Science Teaching* 48, no. 1 (2011): 71–93, doi:10.1002/tea.20386.
8. For more about multimodal representations in PBL, see Suzanne E. Wade and Elizabeth Birr Moje, "The Role of Text in Classroom Learning: Beginning an Online Dialogue," *Reading Online* 5, no. 4 (2001).
9. For NRC and NGSS recommendations regarding simulation use, see National Research Council, *Guide to Implementing the Next Generation Science Standards* (Washington, DC: National Academies Press, 2015); and NGSS Lead States, *Next Generation Science Standards: For States, by States* (Washington, DC: National Academies Press, 2013).
10. For a more extended discussion, see Kathleen Marie Easley, "Simulations and Sensemaking in Elementary Project-Based Science" (PhD diss., University of Michigan, 2020).

Chapter 6

1. See Donella H. Meadows, *Thinking in Systems: A Primer* (White River Junction, VT: Chelsea Green Publishing, 2008).
2. See NGSS Lead States, *Next Generation Science Standards: For States, by States* (Washington, DC: National Academies Press, 2013).
3. For more information about the developmental procedure of the post-unit assessment, see chapter 1.
4. Students receive scores from 0 to 3. Raters were trained to use a rubric to score students' responses and their responses were checked for reliability.
5. For more information about the tug-of-war simulation, see chapter 5.
6. For more information about the ML-PBL curriculum design, see chapter 1.

Chapter 7

1. Joseph Krajcik, Emily Miller, and I-Chien Chen, "Using Project-Based Learning to Leverage Culturally Relevant Pedagogy for Sensemaking of Science in Urban Elementary Classrooms," in *The International Handbook of Research on Multicultural Science Education*, ed. Mary M. Atwater (in press).
2. Melanie M. Cooper, "The Crosscutting Concepts: Critical Component or 'Third Wheel' of Three-Dimensional Learning?" *Journal of Chemistry Education* 97, no. 4 (2020): 903–909, doi:10.1021/acs.jchemed.9b01134; and Jeffrey Nordine and Okhee Lee (eds.), *Crosscutting Concepts: Strengthening Science and Engineering Learning* (Alexandria, VA: National Science Teaching Association, 2021).
3. Joseph Krajcik et al., *Assessing the Effect of Project-Based Learning on Science Learning in Elementary Schools* (technical report, George Lucas Educational Foundation, San Rafael, California, 2020).

Chapter 8

1. All four grade-three units are available on the Lucas Educational Research Sprocket site; request access at https://sprocket.lucasedresearch.org/mlpbl. Addressing literacy standards has become a huge focus for districts across Michigan. With the adoption of the Common Core State Standards (CCSS) for Literacy, and a Read by Grade 3 Law and its assessments, state and regional professional organizations have provided extensive guidance for literacy

instruction and assessment. See National Governors Association Center for Best Practices and Council of Chief State School Officers, *Common Core State Standards for ELA/Literacy* (Washing DC: NGA, 2010); Read by Grade 3 Law information posted on the Michigan Department of Education Academic Standards–Early Literacy web page: https://www.michigan.gov/mde/0,4615,7-140-28753_74161-498394--,00.html; Michigan Association of Intermediate School Administrators General Education Leadership Network Early Literacy Task Force, *Essential Instructional Practices in Early Literacy: K to 3* (Lansing: GELN, 2016), 1–6, https://literacyessentials.org/downloads/gelndocs/k-3_literacy_essentials.pdf; and Nell K. Duke, "Speaking Up for Science and Social Studies," YouTube Video, March 4, 2019, https://www.youtube.com/watch?v=LAWO2lvAnjI. However, not all guidance in Michigan was focused on literacy. Shortly after the new MSS were adopted, the Michigan Department of Education shared a guidance document that promoted integrating science and literacy: Michigan Department of Education, *Supporting Early Literacy Development and Science Instruction* (Lansing: Michigan Department of Education, January 2016), https://www.michigan.gov/documents/mde/Science_and_Literacy_Instruction_in_the_Early_Grades_2_25_16_517048_7.pdf.

2. Jessica Fried-Gaither, *Notable Notebooks: Scientists and Their Writings* (Arlington, VA: NSTA Kids, 2017).
3. Throughout this chapter, certain PBL and lesson features and goals are italicized to highlight how Ms. Hegg incorporated these features in her instruction.
4. Ms. Hegg used the Grade 3 Bookworms Curriculum. OpenUp Resources, *Bookworms ELA Curriculum: K–5 Reading and Writing English Language Curriculum* (Menlo Park, CA: OpenUp Resources, 2018), https://openupresources.org/bookworms-k-5-reading-writing-curriculum/.
5. Bobbie Kalman, *What Is a Biome?* (New York: Crabtree Publishing Company, 1997). Here, relevant general life- and earth-science concepts include migration, predators, biome, climate, ecosystems, environment, and rainforests, as well as descriptions of various habitats.
6. See recommendations for additional read-alouds for ML-PBL's Unit 3.1 at https://docs.google.com/document/d/197_Vlkji5vvsLzB20hxqWI6Far5Sj_HaxJxrDnTbMts/edit. Additional sources for Shared Reading Articles include ReadWorks for Science, Freckle, and Epic.
7. Kate DiCamillo, *Flora and Ulysses: The Illuminated Adventures* (Somerville, MA: Candlewick Press, 2016).
8. Addressing CCSS Grade 3 Integration of Knowledge and Ideas Standards, RL3.7 and RL.3.9.
9. Ms. Hegg's grammar instruction was modeled on recommendations in these resources: Jeff Anderson, *Patterns of Power: Inviting Young Writers into the Conventions of Language, Grades 1–5* (Portsmouth, NH: Stenhouse Publishers, 2017); and OpenUp Resources, *Bookworms ELA Curriculum.*
10. Chris Barton, *Whoosh!: Lonnie Johnson's Super-Soaking Stream of Inventions* (Watertown, MA: Charlesbridge Publishing, Inc., 2016).
11. For more information on literacy in the Toys Unit, see chapter 4, by Miranda S. Fitzgerald and Annemarie Sullivan Palincsar. For read-aloud recommendations for the Toys Unit, including engineering extensions, see https://docs.google.com/document/d/1wfZT7dvd13FvtPQGTQe41ymX1v42j8b_15wr5LfN0cA/edit, addressing CCSS Grade 3 Integration of Knowledge and Ideas Standards, RI.3.9

12. https://docs.google.com/document/d/1wfZT7dvd13FvtPQGTQe41ymX1v42j8b_15wr5Lf N0cA/edit.
13. Cornell Lab, "All About Birds" (website), https://www.allaboutbirds.org/news/.
14. Sneed B. Collard III, *Beaks!* (Watertown, MA: Charlesbridge Publishing, Inc., 2002); and Karen L. Williams and Khadra Mohammed, *Four Feet, Two Sandals* (Grand Rapids, MI: Eerdmans Publishing Company, 2007).
15. For the Birds Unit, recommended titles from the Classroom Library List on Sprocket can be found at https://docs.google.com/document/d/10Q716ZnktLVjRgEcRav7X3NovTj69ELm 0IEX0w_a--Y/edit.
16. Jacqueline Davies, *The Boy Who Drew Birds: The Story of John James Audubon* (Boston: HMH Books, 2004).
17. Narelle Oliver, *Best Beak in Boonaroo Bay* (Golden, CO: Fulcrum Publishing, 1995).
18. Susan Grigsby, *In the Garden with Dr. Carver* (Atlanta: Whitman Publishing, 2010); and Melissa Stewart, *No Monkeys, No Chocolates* (Watertown, MA: Charlesbridge Publishing, Inc., 2018).
19. Titles Ms. Hegg chose to add to the Plants Unit Classroom Library List (https://docs .google.com/document/d/1fqLxzn4dnBN5vfo7am4QgthRg3IiFcUgYE1IcIYx0L0/edit); Lynne Cherry, *How Groundhog's Garden Grew* (New York: Blue Sky Press, 2003); and Eliza Wheeler, *Miss Maple's Seeds* (New York: Nancy Paulsen Books, 2013).
20. Eric R. Banilower et al., *Report of the 2018 National Survey of Science and Math Education* (Chapel Hill, NC: Horizon Research, 2018), http://horizon-research.com/NSSME/2018 -nssme/research-products/reports/technical-report.
21. Michigan Association of Intermediate School Administrators General Education Leadership Network Early Literacy Task Force, *Essential Instructional Practices*, 3–4.
22. Kylene Beers and Robert Probst, *Notice and Note: Strategies for Close Reading* (Portsmouth, NH: Heinemann, 2012); and Kylene Beers and Robert Probst, *Reading Nonfiction: Notice and Note Stances, Signposts, and Strategies* (Portsmouth, NH: Heinemann, 2015).

Chapter 9

1. The teacher preferred that a first-name pseudonym be used in the case.
2. See David Hammer, Fred Goldberg, and Sharon Fargason, "Responsive Teaching and the Beginnings of Energy in a Third Grade Classroom," *Review of Science, Mathematics and ICT Education* 6, no. 1 (2012): 51–72, doi:10.26220/REV.1694.
3. The gender-neutral "Latine" is used as per the preference expressed by the teacher in this case study.
4. Gloria Ladson-Billings, "Toward a Theory of Culturally Relevant Pedagogy," *American Educational Research Journal* 32, no. 3 (1995): 465–491, doi:10.3102/00028312032003465.
5. Joseph S. Krajcik, Emily Miller, and I-Chien Chen, "Using Project-Based Learning to Leverage Culturally Relevant Pedagogy for Sensemaking of Science in Urban Elementary Classrooms," in *The International Handbook of Research on Multicultural Science Education*, ed. Mary M. Atwater (in press).
6. NGSS Lead States, *Next Generation Science Standards: For States, by States* (Washington, DC: National Academies Press, 2013).
7. National Research Council, *A Framework for K–12 Science Education: Practices, Crosscutting Concepts, and Core Ideas* (Washington, DC: National Academies Press, 2012); and NGSS Lead States, *Next Generation Science Standards*.

8. Norma Gonzalez et al., "Funds of Knowledge for Teaching in Latino Households," *Urban Education* 29, no. 4 (1995): 443–470, doi:10.1177/0042085995029004005.
9. Katherine L. McNeill and Leema Berland, "What Is (or Should Be) Scientific Evidence Use in K–12 Classrooms?" *Journal of Research in Science Teaching* 54, no. 5 (2017): 672–689, doi:10.1002/tea.21381.
10. Sneed B. Collard III, *Beaks!* (Watertown, MA: Charlesbridge Publishing, 2002); and Karen L. Williams and Khadra Mohammed, *Four Feet, Two Sandals* (Grand Rapids, MI: Eerdmans Publishing Company, 2007).
11. Sonia Nieto, "Language, Diversity, and Learning: Lessons for Education in the 21st Century," *CAL Digest* (August 2010), https://eclass.upatras.gr/modules/document/file.php/PDE1439/language-diversity-and-learning.pdf.
12. See Phyllis C. Blumenfeld et al., "Motivating Project-Based Learning: Sustaining the Doing, Supporting the Learning," *Educational Psychologist* 26, no. 3–4 (1991): 369–398, doi:10.1207/s15326985ep2603&4_8.
13. Nell K. Duke, Anne-Lise Halvorsen, and Stephanie L. Strachan, "Project-Based Learning Not Just for STEM Anymore," *Phi Delta Kappan* 98, no. 1 (2016): 14–19.
14. Nieto, "Language, Diversity, and Learning."
15. This dialogue was translated from Spanish.
16. See Okhee Lee, Emily Miller, and Rita Januszyk, *NGSS for All Students* (Arlington, VA: NSTA Press, 2015).
17. See Duke, Halvorsen, and Strachan, "Project-Based Learning."
18. The dialogue below was translated from Spanish.

Chapter 10

1. See, for example, Laurie Calvert, "The Power of Teacher Agency: Why We Must Transform Professional Learning So That It Really Supports Educator Learning," *Journal of Staff Development* 37, no. 2 (2016): 51–56, doi:10.1080/13674580500200380.
2. For more on the key features of distributed leadership, see James P. Spillane, Richard Halverson, and John B. Diamond, "Investigating School Leadership Practice: A Distributed Perspective," *Educational Researcher* 30, no. 3 (2001): 23–28, doi:10.3102/0013189X030003023.
3. The sample Driving Question Board in figure 10.1 is a PL session artifact from July 2019.
4. The ML-PBL project refers to "talk moves" as "discourse moves."

Chapter 11

1. See Joseph S. Krajcik, Emily Miller, and I-Chien Chen, "Using Project-Based Learning to Leverage Culturally Relevant Pedagogy for Sensemaking of Science in Urban Elementary Classrooms," in *The International Handbook of Research on Multicultural Science Education*, ed. Mary M. Atwater (in press).
2. See Krajcik et al., *Assessing the Effect of Project-Based Learning on Science Learning in Elementary Schools* (technical report: George Lucas Educational Foundation, San Rafael, California, 2020).
3. See National Research Council, *How People Learn: Brain, Mind, Experience, and School*, vols. 1 and 2 (Washington, DC: National Academies Press, 2000); and Joseph S. Krajcik and Namsoo Shin, "Project-Based Learning," in *The Cambridge Handbook of the Learning Sciences*, ed. R. Keith Sawyer (New York: Cambridge University Press, 2014), 275–297.
4. See Krajcik and Shin, "Project-Based Learning."

5. See Krajcik et al. *Assessing the Effect.*
6. See Rita MacDonald, Sarah Lord, and Emily Miller, *Teaching the Content Areas to English Language Learners in Secondary Schools* (Cham, Switzerland: Springer, 2019).
7. The force and motion simulation is available at https://phet.colorado.edu/en/simulation /forces-and-motion-basics.
8. *Flipbook* was developed by Elliot Soloway and the "Collabrify" team at the University of Michigan and can be accessed at https://techtransfer.umich.edu/companies/collabrify-it/.
9. *WeRead* was also developed by Elliot Soloway and the "Collabrify" team at the University of Michigan and can be accessed at https://techtransfer.umich.edu/companies/collabrify-it/.
10. See Krajcik et al., *Assessing the Effect.*
11. Ibid.

Appendix B

1. Rita MacDonald, Emily Miller, and Sarah Lord, "Doing and Talking Science: Engaging ELs in the Discourse of the Science and Engineering Practices," in *Science Teacher Preparation in Content-Based Second Language Acquisition*, ed. Alandeom W. Oliviera and Molly H. Weinburgh (Cham, Switzerland: Springer, 2017), 179–197.

Acknowledgments

This extensive six-year effort required a range of strengths and could not have been possible without dedicated, knowledgeable, and experienced colleagues who love teaching children science. We benefited greatly from the expertise of teachers and teacher leaders who took risks and moved away from established teaching practices to engage in new practices with the hope of engaging their students in science learning.

As we designed the materials, numerous teachers provided us with excellent feedback on what worked and did not work to engage their students in learning challenging science ideas. Their feedback was indispensable. We would like to thank the following teachers who worked with us during various stages of the development process. (teachers are listed by stage in development cycles and state):

Early Development—Michigan Grade 3 Teachers: Jamie Lehto, Michelle Neelands, Monique Coulman, and Kim Sather (Genesee).

Early Development—Wisconsin Grade 3 Teachers: Stacey Hodkiewicz, Melina Lozano, Mary Modaff, and Alice Severson (Madison).

Field Testing—Michigan Grade 3 Teachers: Margaret Alexander, Norma Balagna, Soni Cummings, Paishann Curtis, Bridget Davidek, Jenny Dumas, Jeremy Garn, Jackie Greenwald, Melissa Iott, Demetria Hoskins, Michelle Householder, Donyelle Johnson, Jonelle Johnston, Becky Joslin, Stacy Kings, Samantha McGregor, Lisa Mereles, Karen Merrell, Rebecca Middleton, Jennifer Morrison, Jill Orr, Brandon Reno, Circe Chavez Rodriguez, Karen Spears, Sherise Timmons.

The ML-PBL team comprises a rich interdisciplinary group of learning scientists, science educators, literacy experts, and quantitative and qualitative researchers—many who were former elementary teachers and all of whom greatly contributed to the design and implementation of ML-PBL. Without the knowledge and dedication of this group, the creative and challenging work we undertook could not have been accomplished. We would like to give a special thanks to Dr. Annemarie Palincsar from the College of Education at the University of Michigan, who served as a co-principal investigator (PI) throughout the project, led the literacy development team, and provided excellent feedback on the cases in this book. We also want to recognize Susan Codere, who served as project manager for ML-PBL throughout the effort and spent countless hours making sure equipment was delivered on time, ensuring teachers were notified, writing detailed reports, and seeing to it that everything occurred according to schedule. Emily Adah Miller, who also served as a co-PI, and Deborah Peek-Brown need to be recognized for their efforts in designing and redesigning the units. Dr. Elliot Soloway from the College of Engineering at the University of Michigan led the technology development efforts; Elliot's RoadMap application became extremely valuable when most schools shifted to virtual environments during the 2020–2021 COVID-19 pandemic. Dr. I-Chien Chen from Michigan State University, who served as a senior data analyst, worked very closely with Barbara to analyze our quantitative data. We owe a special thanks to Dr. Cory Miller—a post-doctoral fellow and research associate at Michigan State University—who, in the early stages of the project, helped to organize files and numerous documents.

Others on the team we would like to thank and recognize include (in alphabetical order) Selin Akgun, Michigan State University (graduate research assistant); Quinton Baker, US Department of Agriculture, formerly Michigan State University (data analyst, graduate research assistant); Kayla Bartz, Michigan State University (data analyst, research assistant); Lydia Bradford, Michigan State University (co-lead data analyst, graduate research assistant); Gabriel Dellavecchia, University of Michigan (graduate research assistant); Kathleen Easley, Learning Partnership, formerly University of Michigan (postdoctoral fellow, graduate research assistant); Dillon Ellsworth, Michigan State University (undergraduate research assistant); Miranda Fitzgerald, University of North Carolina at Charlotte, formerly University of Michigan (postdoctoral fellow, research associate); Chris Klager, Northwestern University formerly Michigan State University (data analyst, graduate research associate); Tingting Li, Michigan State University (graduate research assistant); Josh Meyer, University of Michigan (technology development); Samantha Richar, Michigan State University (graduate research assistant); Robert Ryan, Michigan State University (classroom observer); Gavin Stockton, Michigan State University (undergraduate research assistant); Paul Drummond (classroom observer); and LaDonna White (classroom observer).

We thank as well some previous members of the team:

From Michigan State University: Kellie Finnie, Elli Paulson, Phyllis Pennock, Sam Severance, Sara Severance, and Alex Walus.

From University of Michigan: Kirsten Edwards, Meredith Baker Marcum.

We would also like to give a special thank-you to two of our Madison, Wisconsin teachers who wrote the curriculum alongside us: Alice Severson and Mary Modaff.

We also need to recognize the dedication and service of several staff members and academic specialists from the CREATE for STEM Institute at Michigan State University: Margaret Iding, who helped keep track of the teachers; Mary Luba, who managed our financial records; Ligita Espinosa, who helped to keep Joe focused on his work; Dr. Bob Geier, who provided valuable support in the completion of various documents and IRB applications; and finally, Colter Starr, who helped keep all of our technology working.

Our advisory board members also provided valuable feedback concerning the direction of the project: Dr. Ron Marx, former dean, College of Education, University of Arizona; Dr. Jim Pellegrino, professor, codirector, Learning Science Research Institute, University of Chicago–Illinois; Robby Cramer, retired teacher, executive director, Michigan Science Teacher Association; Dr. Lisa Linnebrink-Garcia, associate professor, Michigan State University; Dr. Rosemary Russ, associate professor, University of Wisconsin–Madison; and Dr. Maria Chiara Simani, executive director, California Science Project, University of California–Davis.

We also give an exceptional thank you to editing consultant Nicole Gallicchio, who spent hours editing the manuscript on a very tight deadline. The book and the cases are more readable because of her focused work.

We are grateful to staff and leadership at Lucas Education Research (LER), a division of the George Lucas Educational Foundation, for their ongoing faith and support in our work to make a difference in the lives of elementary teachers and children. This includes the founding members of LER: Kristin De Vivo (Executive Director), Sheree Santos (Director of Technology Programs), Dr. Angela DeBarger (former Senior Program Officer); Dr. Courtney Paulger (former

Program Officer), Dr. Rochelle Urban (current Program Manager), and Dr. Britte Haugan Cheng (Research Advisor to the Foundation).

We need to give a special thank you to the teachers who are the stars of the case studies. They allowed us into their classrooms as they were learning to teach in a new style and spoke to us extensively about their experiences with ML-PBL. This book could not have been written without the their' dedicated work to enact ML-PBL and concern for improving the lives of elementary students. We want to recognize and give a sincere thanks to:

Danita Byrd (Detroit)
Imelya Eberhardt-Ellison (Detroit)
Jeremy Garn (Carman-Ainsworth)
Lindsey Kramer (Chippewa Valley)
Karen Lavery (Lincoln)
Jamie Lehto (Lincoln)
Melina Lozano (Madison)
Janet Serba (Johannesburg-Lewiston)
Kristine Shrontz (Olivet)

We would also like to recognize other Michigan teachers who were part of the third-grade efficacy study: Holly Berridge, Andrea Berkshire, Brooke Beuschel, Joseph Blauwkamp, Kami Boik, Danita Byrd, Caroline Chuby, Imelya Eberhardt-Ellison, Mindy Geer, Rocio Gomez-Arana, Jacqueline Gorter, Junne Granger, Heather Guerra, Robin Hall, Linnea Hurley, Jennifer Johnson, Tracy King, Arcidevi Kohair, Cacey Kopy, Lindsey Kramer, Beth Lehner, Sarah Lichti, Sherry McKellar, Kari McRaith, Cheryl Mozdrech, Amanda Nolen, Andrew Palma, Simona Pentecost, Amy Popek, Andrea Powers, Valerie Reed, Diana Respecki, Taylor Rich, Heather Roesstorff, Amy Schelhaas, Suzanne Schlachter, Janet Serba, Tammy Singleton, Kristine Shrontz, Kay Shufeldt, Jean Strohpaul, Brock Willemin, Latoya Wilson.

And special thanks go to the many science specialists and teacher leaders who supported this work from the beginning: Danita Byrd, Chiara Kirkland, Darrin Donaldson, James Emmerling, Kellie Finnie, Kristie Ford, Billie Freeland, Julie Hilker, Amy Lazarowicz, Kalonda McDonald, Michelle Neelands, Amber Richmond, Moira Thomas, Jodi Sturk, and Wendi Vogel.

Thank you for believing in the vision of PBL to transform elementary classrooms.

Joe and Barbara
Michigan State University
East Lansing, Michigan
January 20, 2021

About the Editors

Joseph Krajcik serves as director of the CREATE for STEM Institute and is the Lappan-Phillips Professor of Science Education at Michigan State University (MSU). Throughout his career, Krajcik has focused on working with teachers to design and test instructional materials to reform science teaching practices that promote students' engagement in and learning of science. He is currently working on several funded projects to design, develop, and test instructional materials that engage learners through project-based learning (PBL) and that align with the Next Generation Science Standards (NGSS) and the Framework for K–12 Science Education. Krajcik served as lead writer for developing Physical Science Standards for the NGSS and the lead writer for the Physical Science Design team for the Framework for K–12 Science Education. He received the McGraw Prize in 2020 for innovation in education, the George G. Mallinson Award from the Michigan Science Teachers' Association in 2014 for overall excellence of contributions to science education, and the Distinguished Contributions to Science Education Through Research Award in 2010 from NARST. In 2019, he was elected to the National Academy of Education. Prior to receiving his PhD, Joe taught high school chemistry and physical science.

Barbara Schneider is the John A. Hannah University Distinguished Professor in the College of Education and Department of Sociology at MSU. Her research focuses on how the social contexts of schools and families influence adolescents' academic and social well-being as they move into adulthood. Barbara has played a significant role in developing research methods for the real-time measurement of learning experiences in context. She is a Fellow of the American Association for the Advancement of Science, National Academy of Education, and American Educational Research Association. She was recently elected to the Finnish Academy of Science and Letters and received an honorary PhD from the University of Helsinki in 2017. Schneider is the principal investigator of Crafting Engagement in Science Environments, an international study testing the impact of PBL on student academic, social, and emotional factors in high school science classes. She is also the co-principal investigator of a similar initiative at the elementary school level. Schneider has published nineteen books and more than 150 articles and reports on family, the social contexts of schooling, and the sociology of knowledge. Her most recent book is *Learning Science: Crafting Engagement in Science Environment*, published by Yale University Press, 2020.

About the Contributors

Emily C. Adah Miller is the co-principal investigator, senior researcher, lead developer and writer of curriculum, teacher professional learning and assessment on the ML-PBL project, Efficacy Study project, and Understanding Adaptations project. She served as a lead writer for the Diversity and Equity Team on the NGSS, and as a member of the NGSS writing team. Adah Miller has written multiple peer-reviewed articles, the best-selling teacher practice book *NGSS for All*, and the upcoming *Crosscutting Concepts*. Adah Miller holds ESL and bilingual teaching certifications, having taught for two decades in Wisconsin as an ESL and bilingual resource science specialist in Title I schools at the middle and elementary school levels. She received an NSF Teacher Professional Development grant from the Wisconsin Center for Educational Research (WCER). Adah Miller collaborated with WCER to design discourse tools aligned with the English Language Proficiency Development Framework and co-chaired the adoption of the new English Language Development standards in Wisconsin. Her research targets opportunities for sensemaking for underrepresented students in PBL science contexts and how teachers can build on these opportunities. Additional interests include how professional learning for teachers can leverage the building of theory and practice within research–practice partnerships. Adah Miller received her PhD in Curriculum and Instruction from the University of Wisconsin–Madison.

Selin Akgun is a PhD student in the Curriculum, Instruction and Teacher Education program with a concentration in science education at Michigan State University. Currently, she is a research assistant working for the CREATE for STEM Institute on the Multiple Literacies in the Project-Based Learning (ML-PBL) project. Akgun earned her BS and MA in elementary science education from Bogazici University in Turkey. She has worked as an informal science educator and taught middle school science at the Istanbul Technical University Science Center. She has also worked with preservice science teachers and university students from different majors through research projects funded by Bogazici University. Akgun's research interests include supporting students' sensemaking and teachers' teaching practices through project-based learning and their identity construction within the lenses of sociocultural theory; she is also interested in the history and philosophy of science. Her research has been published in the *International Journal of Science Education*, *International Journal of Science and Mathematics Education*, and *Science & Education*.

Kayla Bartz is a third-year PhD student in the Measurement and Quantitative Methods program at Michigan State University, with an undergraduate degree in psychology from North Central College in Illinois. Her research focus is on measurement, which includes survey methodology and development, and on studying the psychometric properties of varying assessments and surveys. Her expertise includes analyses of validity, reliability, and difficulty on standardized achievement tests. Currently, she is conducting a series of analyses on the formative and summative assessments in ML-PBL for the third through the fifth grade. Bartz's publications include "The Relationship Between Teacher's Support of Literacy Development and Elementary Students' Modeling Proficiency in Project-Based Learning Science Classrooms" in the *International Journal of Primary, Elementary and Early Years Education* and "Transition Planning Involvement and Students with Intellectual Disability: Findings from NLTS 2012" in *Career Development and Transition for Exceptional Individuals*. Bartz has received a graduate fellowship from the John A. Hannah Chair for her scholarly productivity.

I-Chien Chen has a PhD in sociology and works as a research associate in the College of Education at Michigan State University. In her research, Chen uses a sociological lens to understand how social contexts, interpersonal relationships, and intervention programs enhance students' educational expectations, college-going decisions, and interest in STEM majors and careers. Her research centers on ways to make educational opportunities, resources, and information accessible to students, particularly those who have historically been underrepresented in the education system. She draws on social-psychological perspectives and sociocultural studies of learning and uses causal inference with social network analysis as a tool to understand students' and teachers' learning behavior.

Chen's articles have been published in numerous peer-reviewed journals, including the *American Educational Research Journal, AERA Open, Journal of Research on Technology in Education, Teachers College Record, Social Science Research,* and *Clinical Psychology Review.* Her research on the use of smartphone technology for enhancing college access for low-income and minority students was recently published in the *Journal of Research on Technology in Education* and in the *International Handbook of Research on Multicultural Science Education.* Chen has received a postdoctoral fellowship from the John A. Hannah Chair in the College of Education at MSU.

Susan Codere is the ML-PBL project director at the CREATE for STEM Institute at Michigan State University, where she manages curriculum development, review, revision, and sharing; professional learning; and research activities. Before joining the ML-PBL team, Codere served as the project coordinator for standards development in the Michigan Department of Education. She served as the Lead State Representative from Michigan on the Next Generation Science Standards (NGSS) development team and coordinated Michigan's NGSS internal review and implementation planning processes. Codere served as the project coordinator for the development and implementation of Michigan's High School Content Expectations in Science, Mathematics, English Language Arts, and Social Studies. She works closely with colleagues across the state to support standards implementation and promotes career and college readiness through literacy across the content areas. Codere holds BS degrees in secondary science education and medical technology from Michigan Technological University and an MS degree in microbiology and immunology from MSU.

Kathleen Marie Easley is a postdoctoral research fellow at the Learning Partnership in Chicago, where she supports curriculum development in inquiry-based science. Her research interests include supporting student collaboration, argumentation, and sensemaking in PBL that integrates science and literacy. Easley holds a PhD from the University of Michigan in educational studies, with a concentration in literacy, language, and culture. While at the University of Michigan, she worked with the ML-PBL project, supporting both curriculum design and professional development. She also taught a literacy methods course for elementary educators. Easley has published on student collaboration in the edited book *Promoting*

Academic Talk in Schools and has another article on student collaboration in *Science and Children* (in press). She has been an author on a National Research Council report on the integration of literacy and science, a chapter on critical socioculturalism for the *Handbook of Educational Psychology* (in press), and an *Oxford Research Encyclopedia of Education* article on teacher education. Before receiving her PhD, Kathleen taught at a Montessori school in Illinois.

Miranda S. Fitzgerald is an assistant professor and a teacher educator at the University of North Carolina at Charlotte, where she teaches and studies elementary literacy instruction and assessment. Her work involves three central concerns: the potential benefits of learning environments that integrate language literacy and science instruction for literacy development and disciplinary knowledge-building; features of instruction that support the development of vocabulary and reading comprehension; and strategies that support pre- and in-service teachers to learn and use research-supported instructional practices in literacy. In 2017, Fitzgerald was awarded the International Literacy Association's Steven A. Stahl Research Grant and an AERA Division C Graduate Student Research Grant to partially fund research for her dissertation, *Texts and Tasks in Elementary Project-Based Science*. For this research, she was the recipient of the 2019 AERA Research in Reading and Literacy SIG's Graduate Student Award for Literacy Excellence and the 2019 University of Michigan School of Education's Stanley E. and Ruth B. Dimond Best Dissertation Award. Her work has been published in the *American Journal of Education*, *International Journal of Educational Research*, *Reading Research Quarterly*, *Reading & Writing Quarterly*, and *Review of Research in Education*. Fitzgerald completed her PhD at the University of Michigan.

Tingting Li is currently a first-year doctoral student in the Educational Psychology and Educational Technology program at Michigan State University. She is also a PhD candidate in the Science Education program at Northeast Normal University in China, where her focus is on chemistry education. Her research interests include promoting K–12 students' deep science learning and engagement with multimedia and assessing students' knowledge-in-use. In 2018, she was awarded a scholarship from the China Scholarship Council's joint doctoral student learning abroad program. Currently, she is a research assistant with the ML-PBL project at the CREATE for STEM Institute at MSU. Li's research has been published in *Chemistry Education Research and Practice*, *Education 3–13:*

International Journal of Primary, Elementary and Early Years Education, and multiple highly ranked Chinese peer-reviewed journals, including the *Chinese Journal of Chemical Education*, *Studies in Foreign Education*, and *Primary & Secondary Schooling Abroad.*

Cory Susanne Miller is a research associate working on the ML-PBL project for the CREATE for STEM Institute at Michigan State University. She is currently working on PBL curriculum development and providing professional learning for K–5 science teachers. Miller earned her PhD in teaching and learning from the University of South Carolina, where she worked in the Center for Science Education providing professional development for middle school science teachers. She has also worked with preservice teachers at the University of South Carolina and the College of Charleston. Her research interests include teacher learning of PBL strategies and the personal processes that lead to changes in practice. Her research has been published in *Research in Science Education.* Before receiving her PhD, Miller taught PreK–7- science in both Connecticut and South Carolina.

Annemarie Sullivan Palincsar is the Ann L. Brown Distinguished University Professor of Education, Jean and Charles Walgreen Jr. Chair of Reading and Literacy, Arthur F. Thurnau Professor, and a teacher educator at the University of Michigan. Palincsar s primary research interest is in sensemaking and knowledge-building with multiple media, especially in the context of project-based scientific inquiry. She has served on a number of task forces and National Research Council panels, including *Preventing Reading Difficulties in Young Children*, *Preparing Future Teachers,* the *RAND Reading Study Group*, and *How People Learn: Volume II.* Palincsar has been active in professional organizations, serving as a member of the Literacy Research Panel for the International Reading Association, executive board member for the National Academy of Education, and member-at-large for the American Educational Research Association. She also is a member of the National Academy of Education and is an American Educational Research Association Fellow. She was the co-editor of *Cognition and Instruction.* Her research has been published in *Journal of the Learning Sciences*, *Educational Researcher*, *Harvard Education Review*, *Linguistics and Education*, *Teaching and Teacher Education*, and *Reading and Writing Quarterly*, among others. Annemarie completed her PhD at the University of Illinois.

Deborah Peek-Brown is an academic outreach specialist for the Create for STEM Institute at Michigan State University. She is currently part of K–5 science curriculum project teams that design, develop, and test instructional materials that align with the NGSS. Her expertise and research interests include engaging students through PBL, science literacy, and the development of comprehensive professional learning programs for teachers. Peek-Brown began her career as a science educator in Detroit Public Schools, where she taught, supported teachers, developed curriculum materials, and planned districtwide professional development programs for twenty-eight years. In 2016, she also worked as the acting executive director of the district's Office of Science, where she coordinated all K–12 science education curricula and programs. She has been a longstanding board member of the Michigan Science Teachers' Association and was awarded the George G. Mallinson Award for overall excellence of contributions to science education in 2018. Peek-Brown has presented at local, national, and international education conferences, including the annual meetings of the Michigan Science Teachers Association, National Science Teaching Association, NARST, European Science Education Research Association, and International Conference of the Learning Sciences.

Index